THE BOOK OF

FONDUES

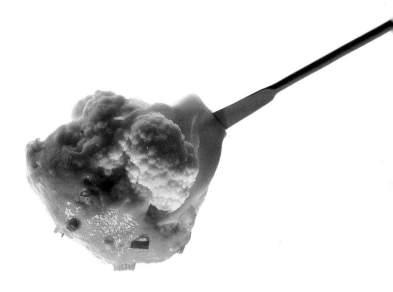

T H E   B O O K   O F

FONDUES

LORNA RHODES

Photography by
SIMON BUTCHER

a Salamander book
Published by Salamander Books Limited
LONDON • NEW YORK

Published 1987 by Salamander Books Ltd,
129-137 York Way, London N7 9LG
By arrangement with Merehurst Press,
5 Great James Street, London WC1N 3DA

©Copyright Merehurst Limited 1987

ISBN: 0 86101 715 3

Managing Editor: Felicity Jackson
Editor: Louise Steele
Designer: Roger Daniels
Home Economist: Lorna Rhodes
Photographer: Simon Butcher
Typeset by Angel Graphics
Colour separation by J. Film Process Ltd, Bangkok, Thailand.
Printed in Belgium by Proost International Book Production

ACKNOWLEDGEMENTS

The Publishers would like to thank the following for their
help and advice:
China supplied by Chinacraft of London, 499 Oxford Street,
London W1 and branches
David Mellor, 26 James Street, Covent Garden, London WC2E 8PA,
4 Sloane Square, London SW1W 8EE and
66 King Street, Manchester M2 4NP
Elizabeth David Limited, 46 Bourne Street, London SW1 and at
Covent Garden Kitchen Supplies, 3 North Row, The Market,
London WC2
Neal Street East, the Oriental specialist, 5 Neal Street,
Covent Garden, London WC2
Philips Home Appliances, City House, 420-430 London Road,
Croydon CR9 3QR

FRONT COVER RECIPES (top to bottom)
Spicy Prawns, see page 47
Chinese Seafood Hotpot, see page 58
Strawberry Roulé Dip, see page 66
Leek Purée, see page 63

CONTENTS

INTRODUCTION

A fondue party is a really enjoyable way to entertain informally. What's more, the preparation is done in advance, leaving the hostess free to relax and enjoy a leisurely meal with her guests.

The Book of Fondues contains over 100 delicious recipes with a truly international flavour, plus lots of exciting ideas for foods to dip and many unusual accompaniments.

A wide variety of cheeses has been used to create deliciously-different cheese fondues from around the world, including the Classic Swiss Fondue (a wonderful mixture of melted Emmental and Gruyère cheeses, and wine), as well as an unusual Fondue Normande – a mouthwatering creation of Camembert, Calvados brandy, wine and cream.

The other most popular type of fondue uses hot oil to cook the food – and recipes in this section include the all-time favourite Fondue Bourguignonne, plus other innovative ideas such as Fruity Duck Fondue and Veal Milanese.

You will also find succulent Wafer-Wrapped Prawns and Seafood Tempura (just two ideas from the Seafood Fondue selection) and some exotic Hotpots, which use simmering chicken stock, instead of oil, to cook the foods. There are also lots of tasty vegetarian dishes and a wonderfully-tempting choice of Sweet Fondues.

Illustrated throughout with colourful and informative step-by-step photographs, here is a wonderful collection of recipes and ideas to delight fondue-cooks and party guests for many years to come.

FONDUE EQUIPMENT

There are many types of fondue sets on the market – they all contain a pot; a stand, on which the pot rests, and a burner for cooking or keeping the food hot.

The earthenware or pottery pots resemble the original Swiss caquelon and are used for cheese fondues. These are wide and shallow in shape and designed specifically to allow room for easy swirling of foods into the melted cheese mixture. (Do not attempt to use these pots for hot oil fondues.)

When preparing a cheese fondue, you may find the mixture forms a soft, dough-like ball in the centre of the liquor. Don't worry, this is quite normal and you will find it gradually melts to form a smooth mixture. Whatever you do, don't be tempted to raise the heat and try to hurry the melting process along, or you will overcook and spoil the mixture. It is essential to keep the prepared melted cheese fondue over the right degree of heat, and frequent stirring is essential to keep the mixture smooth and prevent it burning. This is done as guests dip and swirl items of food on fondue forks or skewers. When the cheese fondue is almost finished, the mixture at the base of the pot will have formed a crust – this is delicious and should be scraped out and divided among the guests.

The enamelled cast iron or metal pots are used for the popular hot oil fondues, such as Fondue Bourguignonne. These pots may also be used for cheese and dessert fondues, provided the heat is kept low. To prepare a hot oil fondue, fill the pot one-third full with vegetable oil and heat it on the kitchen hob until it reaches 190C (375F). Then, very carefully, transfer the pot to the burner in the centre of the dining table.

The hot oil fondue pot is a versatile piece of equipment and also lends itself to cooking dishes like hotpots, which use simmering stock to cook the food.

Mongolian Hotpot is traditionally cooked in a special pot with a built in chimney in the centre, but if you do not have one, a hot oil fondue pot can be used instead. With this dish, as the items of food cook, the stock becomes richer and more flavourful and is finally served as a soup – once the dipping and cooking is completed.

The small fondue pots are used for desserts and the candle burner is adequate for keeping the sauce warm.

In addition to the fondue pot, stand and burner, you will need long-handled fondue forks or bamboo skewers to spear the foods for dipping and cooking. Chinese wire strainers are recommended in some cases – for convenience and safety – and these are available from cook shops and Chinese supermarkets.

When cooking hot oil fondues or recipes for hotpots, place the fondue pot of hot oil, or simmering stock, in the centre of the table. Arrange place settings of dinner plates or bowls and 'eating' forks on the table with the accompanying platters of foods to be cooked, plus dipping sauces, accompaniments, salads and so on. Then let guests help themselves. To cook meat, fish or vegetables, simply thread a piece of food onto a fondue fork or bamboo skewer (or preferably a Chinese wire strainer for hotpots) and immerse food into hot oil (or stock). Once cooked to your liking, the food is then transferred to the dinner plate and dipped into one of the sauces with an 'eating' fork, while the next cube of meat, fish or vegetable is cooking on the fondue fork. Remember that if too much food is added to the hot oil at one time it causes the temperature to drop and it will need reheating again on the kitchen hob. You may like to have a plate lined with absorbent kitchen paper handy on the table for draining cooked foods before eating – especially for any battered or crumbed items.

CLASSIC SWISS FONDUE

1 clove garlic, halved
250 ml (8 fl oz/1 cup) dry white wine
1 teaspoon lemon juice
250 g (8 oz/2 cups) grated Gruyère cheese
250 g (8 oz/2 cups) grated Emmental cheese
2 teaspoons cornflour
2 tablespoons kirsch
pinch of white pepper
pinch of freshly grated nutmeg
cubes of French bread, to serve

Rub the inside of the fondue pot with cut clove of garlic.

Pour in wine and lemon juice and heat gently until bubbling. Reduce the heat to low and gradually stir in grated cheeses with a wooden spoon, then continue to heat until cheeses melt, stirring frequently.

In a small bowl, blend cornflour smoothly with kirsch, then stir into cheese mixture and continue to cook for 2-3 minutes until mixture is thick and smooth, stirring frequently. Do not allow fondue to boil. Season with pepper and nutmeg. Serve with cubes of French bread.

Serves 4-6.

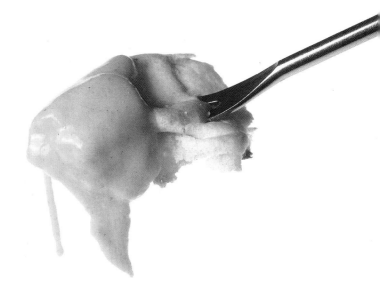

CURRIED CHEESE FONDUE

1 clove garlic, halved
155 ml (5 fl oz/²⁄₃ cup) dry white wine
1 teaspoon lemon juice
2 teaspoons curry paste
250 g (8 oz/2 cups) grated Gruyère cheese
185 g (6 oz/1½ cups) grated Cheddar cheese
1 teaspoon cornflour
2 tablespoons dry sherry
pieces of Nan bread, to serve

Rub the inside of the fondue pot with cut clove of garlic.

Pour in wine and lemon juice and heat gently until bubbling. Reduce the heat to low, add curry paste and gradually stir in grated cheeses, then continue to heat until cheeses melt, stirring frequently.

In a small bowl, blend cornflour smoothly with sherry, then stir into cheese mixture and continue to cook for 2-3 minutes until mixture is thick and smooth, stirring frequently. Do not allow fondue to boil. Serve with pieces of Nan bread.

Serves 4-6.

SOMERSET FONDUE

½ a small onion
250 ml (8 fl oz/1 cup) dry cider
1 teaspoon lemon juice
375 g (12 oz/3 cups) grated Cheddar cheese
½ teaspoon dry mustard
3 teaspoons cornflour
3 tablespoons apple juice
pinch of white pepper
wedges of apple and cubes of crusty bread, to serve

Rub the inside of the fondue pot with cut side of onion.

Pour in cider and lemon juice and heat gently until bubbling. Reduce the heat to low and gradually stir in grated cheese, then continue to heat until cheese melts, stirring frequently.

In a small bowl, blend mustard and cornflour smoothly with apple juice. Stir into cheese mixture and continue to cook for 2-3 minutes until mixture is thick and creamy, stirring frequently. Season with pepper. Serve with wedges of apple and cubes of crusty bread.

Serves 4-6.

SMOKY GERMAN FONDUE

½ a small onion
250 ml (8 fl oz/1 cup) light ale
375 g (12 oz/3 cups) grated German smoked cheese
125 g (4 oz/1 cup) grated Emmental cheese
3 teaspoons cornflour
3 tablespoons milk
1 teaspoon German mustard
rye bread and cooked frankfurters, to serve

Rub the inside of the fondue pot with cut side of onion.

Pour in ale and heat gently until bubbling. Reduce the heat to low and gradually stir in the grated cheeses, then continue to heat until cheeses melt, stirring frequently.

In a small bowl, blend cornflour smoothly with milk, stir into cheese with mustard and continue to cook for 2-3 minutes until mixture is thick and creamy, stirring frequently. Serve with cubes of rye bread and pieces of cooked frankfurters.

Serves 4-6.

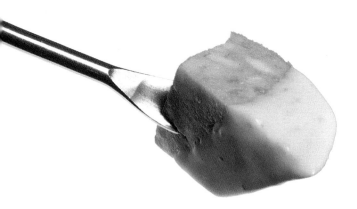

BLUE CHEESE FONDUE

250 ml (8 fl oz/1 cup) milk
250 g (8 oz/1 cup) cream cheese
250 g (8 oz/2 cups) grated Danish Blue cheese
½ teaspoon garlic salt
3 teaspoons cornflour
2 tablespoons single (light) cream
cubes of ham or garlic sausage and cubes of crusty
    bread, to serve

Put milk and cream cheese into the fondue
pot and with an electric mixer, beat until
creamy and smooth.

Place fondue pot over a gentle heat and
gradually stir in the blue cheese, then
continue to heat until smooth, stirring.

Blend garlic salt and cornflour smoothly with
cream; stir into cheese and cook for a further
2-3 minutes until thick and creamy, stirring
frequently. Serve with cubes of ham or garlic
sausage and cubes of crusty bread.

Serves 4-6.

CHEESE & ONION FONDUE

30 g (1 oz/6 teaspoons) butter
1 large onion, very finely chopped
2 teaspoons plain flour
155 ml (5 fl oz/²⁄₃ cup) thick sour cream
250 g (8 oz/2 cups) grated Gruyère cheese
250 g (8 oz/2 cups) grated Cheddar cheese
2 tablespoons chopped fresh chives
pepper
small cooked potatoes and small cooked sausages, to serve

Melt butter in a saucepan, add onion and cook for 4-5 minutes until soft but not brown.

Stir in flour, then add thick sour cream and cook for 2 minutes. Continue to cook whilst adding cheeses and heat until mixture is smooth, stirring frequently.

Add chives and season with pepper. Pour into the fondue pot and serve with small cooked potatoes and small cooked sausages.

Serves 4-6.

FONDUE ITALIENNE

1 clove garlic, halved
315 ml (10 fl oz/1¼ cups) milk
250 g (8 oz/2 cups) grated Mozzarella cheese
250 g (8 oz) Dolcelatte cheese, chopped
60 g (2 oz/½ cup) finely grated Parmesan cheese
2 teaspoons cornflour
3 tablespoons dry white wine
salami, bread sticks and olives, to serve

Rub the inside of the fondue pot with cut clove of garlic. Add milk and heat until bubbling.

Stir in all the cheeses and continue to heat until melted, stirring frequently.

Blend cornflour smoothly with wine, stir into cheese mixture and cook for 2-3 minutes until thick and creamy, stirring frequently. Serve with slices of rolled up salami or cubes of salami, bread sticks and olives.

Serves 4-6.

DUTCH FONDUE

½ a small onion
250 ml (8 fl oz/1 cup) milk
500 g (1 lb/4 cups) grated Gouda cheese
2 teaspoons caraway seeds
3 teaspoons cornflour
3 tablespoons gin
pepper
light rye bread and button mushrooms, to serve

Rub the inside of the fondue pot with cut side of onion.

Add milk and heat until bubbling, then gradually stir in cheese. Continue to heat until cheese melts, stirring frequently.

Stir in caraway seeds. In a small bowl, blend cornflour smoothly with gin, then stir into cheese mixture and cook for 2-3 minutes until smooth and creamy, stirring frequently. Season with pepper. Serve with cubes of rye bread and mushrooms.

Serves 4-6.

PLOUGHMAN'S FONDUE

1 clove garlic, halved
315 ml (10 fl oz/1¼ cups) beer
250 g (8 oz/2 cups) grated Red Leicester cheese
    or orange-coloured Cheddar
250 g (8 oz/2 cups) grated Cheddar cheese
3 teaspoons plain flour
1 teaspoon dry mustard
pepper
cubes of granary or white bread and pickles, to serve

Rub the inside of the fondue pot with cut clove of garlic. Add beer and heat until bubbling.

Toss grated cheeses in the flour and mustard until well combined.

Over a low heat, add cheeses to the beer and continue to heat, stirring all the time until mixture is smooth. Season with pepper. Serve with cubes of granary or white bread and pickles.

Serves 4-6.

ROSÉ FONDUE

1 clove garlic, halved
250 ml (8 fl oz/1 cup) rosé wine
125 g (4 oz/1 cup) grated Gruyère cheese
250 g (8 oz/2 cups) grated red-veined Cheddar cheese
3 teaspoons cornflour
2 tablespoons kirsch
cubes of sesame-coated French bread, to serve

Rub the inside of the fondue pot with cut clove of garlic. Add wine and heat until bubbling.

Gradually stir in cheeses and continue to heat gently until melted, stirring frequently.

In a small bowl, blend cornflour smoothly with kirsch and stir into cheese mixture. Cook for 2-3 minutes until smooth and thickened, stirring frequently. Serve with cubes of French bread.

Serves 4-6.

CRICKETER'S FONDUE

15 g (½ oz/3 teaspoons) butter
1 small onion, finely chopped
250 ml (8 fl oz/1 cup) light ale
500 g (1 lb/4 cups) grated Lancashire cheese
4 teaspoons cornflour
5 tablespoons single (light) cream
cauliflower flowerets, radishes and mushrooms, to
  serve

Heat butter in a saucepan, add onion and cook gently until soft. Pour in ale and heat until bubbling.

Over a low heat, stir in the cheese and continue to heat until cheese has melted, stirring frequently.

In a small bowl, blend cornflour smoothly with cream, add to cheese mixture and cook for 2-3 minutes until smooth and thickened, stirring frequently. Pour into a fondue pot. Serve with cauliflower flowerets, radishes and mushrooms.

Serves 4-6.

DANISH FONDUE

185 g (6 oz) lean middle bacon, rind removed
    and finely chopped
1 small onion, finely chopped
15 g (½ oz/3 teaspoons) butter
3 teaspoons plain flour
250 ml (8 fl oz/1 cup) lager
250 g (8 oz/2 cups) grated Havarti cheese
250 g (8 oz/2 cups) grated Samso cheese
small sweet and sour gherkins and chunks of light rye
    bread, to serve

Put bacon, onion and butter into a saucepan
and cook until bacon is golden and onion is
soft.

Stir in flour, then gradually add lager and
cook until thickened, stirring frequently.

Add cheeses, stirring all the time, and
continue cooking until cheeses have melted
and mixture is smooth. Pour into a fondue
pot and serve with gherkins and chunks of
light rye bread.

Serves 4-6.

ISRAELI FONDUE

2 avocados, halved and stoned
3 teaspoons lemon juice
1 clove garlic, halved
185 ml (6 fl oz/¾ cup) dry white wine
375 g (12 oz/3 cups) grated Edam cheese
2 teaspoons cornflour
5 tablespoons smetana or thick sour cream
cubes of sesame-coated French bread and red and green
    pepper (capsicum), to serve

Scoop out flesh from avocados into a bowl
and mash until smooth with lemon juice.

Rub the inside of fondue pot with cut side of
garlic, then pour in wine and heat until
bubbling. Over a gentle heat, stir in cheese
and cook until melted, stirring frequently.

In a small bowl, blend cornflour smoothly
with smetana or sour cream, then add to
cheese mixture with mashed avocados.
Continue to cook for 4-5 minutes until thick
and smooth, stirring frequently. Serve with
cubes of bread and red and green pepper
(capsicum).

Serves 4-6.

FONDUE NORMANDE

1 clove garlic, halved
125 ml (4 fl oz/½ cup) dry white wine
155 ml (5 fl oz/⅔ cup) single (light) cream
375 g (12 oz) Camembert cheese, rind removed
3 teaspoons cornflour
4 tablespoons Calvados brandy
cubes of French bread and chunks of apple, to serve

Rub the inside of fondue pot with cut side of garlic. Pour in wine and cream and heat until bubbling.

Cut cheese into small pieces, then add to the pot and stir over a gentle heat until melted.

In a small bowl, blend cornflour smoothly with Calvados, then add to cheese mixture and continue to cook for 2-3 minutes until thick and creamy, stirring frequently. Serve with cubes of French bread and chunks of apple.

Serves 4-6.

HIGHLAND FONDUE

1 small onion, finely chopped
15 g (½ oz/3 teaspoons) butter
250 ml (8 fl oz/1 cup) milk
500 g (1 lb/4 cups) grated Scottish or mature Cheddar
  cheese
3 teaspoons cornflour
4 tablespoons whisky
cubes of rye and onion bread, to serve

Put onion and butter into a saucepan and cook over a gentle heat until soft. Add milk and heat until bubbling.

Gradually stir in cheese and continue to cook until melted, stirring frequently.

In a small bowl, blend cornflour smoothly with whisky, then stir into cheese mixture and cook 2-3 minutes until thickened, stirring frequently. Pour into the fondue pot and serve with cubes of rye and onion bread.

Serves 4-6.

WELSH FONDUE

30 g (1 oz/6 teaspoons) butter
250 g (8 oz) leeks, trimmed and finely chopped
6 teaspoons plain flour
250 ml (8 fl oz/1 cup) lager
315 g (10 oz/2½ cups) grated Caerphilly cheese
pepper
cubes of crusty bread, to serve

Put butter into a saucepan and melt over a
low heat. Add leeks, cover pan and cook
gently for 10 minutes until tender.

Stir in flour and cook for 1 minute, then add
lager and heat until thickened, stirring all the
time.

Gradually add cheese and continue to cook
until melted, stirring frequently. Season with
pepper. Pour into a fondue pot and serve with
cubes of crusty bread.

Serves 4-6.

CELEBRATION FONDUE

1 clove garlic, halved
250 ml (8 fl oz/1 cup) sparkling white wine
125 g (4 oz/1 cup) grated Emmental cheese
375 g (12 oz/3 cups) grated Saint Paulin cheese
2 egg yolks
4 tablespoons single (light) cream
2 teaspoons cornflour
2 tablespoons brandy
Bresaola and cubes of French bread, to serve

Rub the inside of fondue pot with cut clove of garlic. Add wine and heat until bubbling.

Gradually add cheeses and heat until melting, then beat in egg yolks and cream.

In a small bowl, blend cornflour smoothly with brandy, then add to cheese mixture and continue to cook, stirring all the time, until the fondue is thick and creamy. Serve with rolls of Bresaola and cubes of bread.

Serves 4-6.

— DEVILLED CHEESE FONDUE —

1 clove garlic, halved
185 ml (6 fl oz/¾ cup) milk
375 g (12 oz/3 cups) grated Applewood smoked
  Cheddar cheese
6 teaspoons plain flour
1 teaspoon prepared mustard
2 teaspoons Worcestershire sauce
2 teaspoons horseradish relish
cubes of ham and toasted granary bread, to serve

Rub the inside of the fondue pot with the cut clove of garlic, then add milk and heat until bubbling.

Toss cheese in flour, then add to the pot and stir all the time over a low heat until it is melted and mixture is thick and smooth.

Stir in mustard, Worcestershire sauce and horseradish relish. Serve with cubes of ham and cubes of toasted granary bread.

Serves 4-6.

— FONDUE BOURGUIGNONNE —

1 kg (2 lb) fillet steak

TOMATO SAUCE: 1 tablespoon oil
2 shallots, finely chopped
1 clove garlic, crushed
440 g (14 oz) can chopped tomatoes
2 tablespoons tomato purée (paste)
salt and pepper
1 tablespoon chopped fresh parsley

To make tomato sauce, heat oil in a saucepan, add shallots and cook gently until soft.

Stir in garlic, tomatoes with their juice and tomato purée (paste). Season with salt and pepper, bring to the boil, then reduce heat and simmer, uncovered, for about 30 minutes or until sauce has reduced and thickened. Stir in parsley and serve hot or cold.

Cut the steak into 2.5 cm (1 in) cubes and put into a serving dish. Each person spears a cube of meat with a fondue fork and immerses the meat in the hot oil to fry. The meat cube is cooked according to individual taste.

Serves 4-6.

Note: Serve also with Horseradish Sauce, see page 40; Mustard Sauce, see page 41; Garlic Sauce, see page 55 and Cool Curry Dip, see page 56.

BACON PARCELS

375 g (12 oz) streaky bacon, rinds removed
250 g (8 oz) chicken livers

DEVILLED SAUCE: 15 g (½ oz) butter
1 shallot, finely chopped
3 teaspoons plain flour
155 ml (5 fl oz/⅔ cup) chicken stock
4 tomatoes, skinned and chopped
1 tablespoon tomato purée (paste)
2 teaspoons sugar
1 tablespoon red wine vinegar
3 teaspoons Worcestershire sauce
½ teaspoon paprika
pinch of cayenne pepper

Cut rashers in half; cut livers into pieces.

Wrap bacon around chicken livers and spear onto bamboo skewers Place on a serving plate.

To make devilled sauce, melt butter in a saucepan, add shallot and cook until soft. Stir in flour, then add stock and remaining ingredients. Simmer for 15 minutes, then strain sauce and serve hot with the bacon parcels cooked in the hot oil.

Serves 4.

Note: Serve also with Creamy Onion Sauce, see page 53.

VEAL MILANESE

750 g (1½ lb) leg veal, cubed
3 tablespoons seasoned plain flour
3 eggs, beaten
125 g (4 oz/1 cup) dry breadcrumbs
2 teaspoons finely grated lemon peel

ITALIAN SAUCE: 2 tablespoons olive oil
1 onion, finely chopped
1-2 cloves garlic, crushed
750 g (1½ lb) ripe tomatoes, skinned and chopped
5 tablespoons dry white wine
salt and pepper
1 tablespoon chopped fresh basil

Toss veal in flour; dip in egg and coat in mixed crumbs and peel.

To make Italian sauce, heat oil in a saucepan, add onion and garlic and cook over a low heat until soft. Add tomatoes and wine and season with salt and pepper. Simmer for 30 minutes.

Purée sauce in a blender or food processor until smooth, or press through a sieve. Stir in basil and reheat sauce before serving. Serve with the veal cooked in hot oil.

Serves 4-6.

Note: Serve also with Lemon Parsley Sauce, see page 45, omitting fish stock and using chicken stock instead.

SPICY CHICKEN FONDUE

6 boned and skinned chicken breasts
4 tablespoons oil
2 teaspoons paprika
½ teaspoon chilli powder

CURRY SAUCE: 1 tablespoon oil
1 onion, finely chopped
2 teaspoons mild curry powder
3 teaspoons plain flour
315 ml (10 fl oz/1¼ cups) milk
6 teaspoons mango chutney
salt and pepper

Cut chicken into 2 cm (¾ in) pieces and mix with oil, paprika and chilli powder.

Place chicken on a serving plate. To make curry sauce, heat oil in a saucepan, add onion and cook until soft. Stir in curry powder and cook for 2 minutes, then stir in flour.

Gradually stir in milk and bring slowly to the boil, stirring all the time. Continue to cook until sauce thickens. Simmer for 5 minutes, then add chutney and season with salt and pepper. Serve hot with the chicken cooked in the hot oil.

Serves 4-6.

Note: Serve also with Cucumber Yogurt Sauce, see page 41.

FRUITY DUCK FONDUE

750 g (1½ lb) duck breast fillets, cut in pieces
6 teaspoons seasoned flour
1 teaspoon five-spice powder

MARMALADE SAUCE: 1 tablespoon demerara sugar
155 ml (5 fl oz/⅔ cup) orange juice
4 tablespoons mature orange marmalade
juice of 1 lemon
60 g (2 oz/⅓ cup) raisins, chopped if large

WINE AND CHERRY SAUCE: 1 tablespoon sugar
375 g (12 oz) can black cherries, drained
90 ml (3 fl oz/⅓ cup) red wine
pinch of mixed spice

Toss duck in flour and five-spice powder.

Place duck on a serving plate. To make marmalade sauce, put all the ingredients into a small saucepan and simmer for 5 minutes.

To make wine and cherry sauce. Put all ingredients into a saucepan and simmer for 15 minutes. Press through a sieve, discarding the stones. Serve sauces warm with the duck cooked in the hot oil.

Serves 4.

Note: Serve also with Ginger Sauce, see page 59.

— CHEESY MEATBALL FONDUE —

750 g (1½ lb) lean minced beef
1 tablespoon finely chopped onion
30 g (1 oz/½ cup) fresh wholemeal breadcrumbs
salt and pepper
125 g (4 oz) Cheddar cheese, diced

TANGY SAUCE: 1 tablespoon tomato purée (paste)
1 tablespoon red wine vinegar
2 tablespoons honey
2 teaspoons dry mustard
1 tablespoon Worcestershire sauce
315 ml (10 fl oz/1¼ cups) chicken stock
2 teaspoons cornflour
juice of 1 orange

Mix together beef, onion and breadcrumbs.

Season meat mixture with salt and pepper and divide into 30 balls. Flatten each ball out, place a piece of cheese in centre, then mould meat around cheese, sealing it well to enclose cheese completely.

To make tangy sauce, put tomato purée (paste), wine vinegar, honey, mustard, Worcestershire sauce and stock into a saucepan and simmer for 10 minutes. Blend cornflour smoothly with orange juice, then stir into the sauce and simmer for 1 minute, stirring all the time. Serve with the meatballs cooked in the hot oil.

Serves 6.

Note: Serve also with Relish Sauce, see page 35.

MINCED LAMB FONDUE

625 g (1 ¼ lb) minced lean lamb
3 spring onions, finely chopped
60 g (2 oz/1 cup) fresh breadcrumbs
2 tablespoons chopped fresh parsley
salt and pepper

MUSHROOM SAUCE: 60 g (2 oz/¼ cup) butter
185 g (6 oz) mushrooms, finely chopped
6 teaspoons plain flour
315 ml (10 fl oz/1¼ cups) milk
1 tablespoon dry sherry

Put all the ingredients for the lamb balls into a bowl. Season with salt and pepper and mix together.

With wetted hands, shape mixture into 20-24 balls, the size of a walnut, and place on a serving plate.

To make mushroom sauce, melt butter in a saucepan, add mushrooms and cook gently for 5 minutes. Stir in flour, then slowly add milk and bring to the boil, stirring. Simmer for a further 5 minutes, then season with salt and pepper and add sherry. Serve warm with the lamb balls cooked in the hot oil.

Serves 4-6.

Note: Serve also with Devilled Sauce, see page 29.

CRISPY SAUSAGE BITES

500 g (1 lb) pork sausagemeat
1 small onion, finely chopped
90 g (3 oz/⅓ cup) cream cheese
1 tablespoon chopped fresh parsley
1 teaspoon prepared mustard
30 g (1 oz/½ cup) fresh breadcrumbs
salt and pepper
2 eggs, beaten
90 g (3 oz/¾ cup) dry breadcrumbs

RELISH SAUCE: Tomato Sauce, see page 28
2 tablespoons sweet pickle relish

Put sausagemeat and onion into a frying pan;
cook until lightly brown and crumbly.

Turn into a bowl and add cream cheese,
parsley, mustard, fresh breadcrumbs and
season with salt and pepper. Shape into 16-20
small firm balls, moulding to make them
smooth. Dip first in beaten egg, then roll in
dry breadcrumbs until evenly coated. Chill
until required.

To make relish sauce, put tomato sauce in a
saucepan, stir in relish and heat through.
Serve warm. Each person spears a sausage ball
with a fondue fork and immerses it in the hot
oil to fry until crisp and golden.

Serves 4.

— MIDDLE EASTERN FONDUE —

750 g (1½ lb) lean leg of lamb, cubed

MARINADE: 3 tablespoons olive oil
1 tablespoon lemon juice
1 clove garlic, crushed
1 tablespoon chopped fresh mint
1 teaspoon ground cinnamon
salt and pepper

APRICOT SAUCE: 1 tablespoon oil
1 shallot, finely chopped
440 g (14 oz) can apricots in natural juice
1 tablespoon chopped fresh parsley

Mix marinade ingredients together and pour over cubed lamb.

Cover lamb mixture and leave to marinate for at least 2 hours, or preferably overnight. To make apricot sauce, heat oil in a saucepan, add shallot and cook over a low heat until soft. Add apricots and the juice and simmer for 5 minutes.

Purée sauce in a blender or food processor, then season with salt and pepper and stir in parsley. Reheat before serving. Remove lamb from marinade and arrange on a serving plate when ready to serve and cook in the hot oil.

Serves 4.

Note: Serve also with Cucumber Yogurt Sauce, see page 41.

MEXICAN FONDUE

1 kg (2 lb) lean rump steak

MEXICAN SAUCE: 1 tablespoon oil
½ a Spanish onion, finely chopped
1 clove garlic, crushed
440 g (14 oz) can tomatoes
2 tablespoons tomato purée (paste)
½ teaspoon chilli powder
1 fresh green chilli, seeded and finely chopped
salt and pepper

Cut meat into 2.5 cm (1 in) cubes and put onto a serving plate.

To make Mexican sauce, heat oil in a saucepan, add onion and garlic and cook gently until softened. Stir in tomatoes and their juice, tomato purée (paste) and chilli powder. Simmer, uncovered, for 10 minutes.

Remove sauce from heat and purée in a blender or food processor until smooth, or press through a sieve to give a smooth sauce. Return to the heat, add chopped chilli and simmer for a further 15 minutes. Season with salt and pepper. Serve with the meat cooked in the hot oil.

Serves 4-6.

Note: Serve also with Cool Avocado Dip, see page 40.

PORK SATAY

½ teaspoon chilli powder
1 teaspoon ground coriander
½ teaspoon turmeric
3 teaspoons oil
3 teaspoons soy sauce
½ teaspoon salt
1 kg (2 lb) pork fillet, cubed

PEANUT SAUCE: 60 g (2 oz/⅔ cup) desiccated coconut
315 ml (10 fl oz/1¼ cups) boiling water
5 tablespoons crunchy peanut butter
2 teaspoons sugar
1 fresh green chilli, seeded and finely chopped
1 teaspoon lemon juice
1 clove garlic, crushed

In a bowl, mix together spices, oil, soy sauce and salt to make a paste. Add pork and with wet hands, knead paste into meat. Cover bowl and leave in the refrigerator for at least 2 hours.

To make peanut sauce, put coconut into a bowl, pour over boiling water and leave to stand for 15 minutes. Strain mixture into a saucepan, pressing well to extract all moisture. Discard coconut. Add remaining ingredients and mix well. Cook over a low heat, stirring until the sauce comes to the boil. Serve hot with the meat cooked in hot oil.

Serves 4-6.

TERIYAKI FONDUE

1 kg (2 lb) fillet steak
3 teaspoons light soft brown sugar
125 ml (4 fl oz/½ cup) soy sauce
6 tablespoons dry sherry
2 cloves garlic, crushed
1 teaspoon ground ginger

BEANSPROUT SALAD: 1 small head Chinese leaves
250 g (8 oz) fresh beansprouts
1 red pepper (capsicum), seeded and finely sliced
½ bunch spring onions, shredded
6 tablespoons sunflower oil
1 tablespoon wine vinegar

Cut steak into thin strips 1 cm (½ in) wide
and 10 cm (4 in) long.

Put 1 teaspoon of sugar and 2 tablespoons of
soy sauce into a bowl and set aside. In a large
bowl, combine remaining sugar and soy
sauce, sherry, garlic and ginger. Add strips of
meat and leave to marinate for 1 hour. Weave
the strips of meat onto 20-24 bamboo skewers
ready for cooking in hot oil.

To prepare the salad, shred Chinese leaves
and put into a bowl with beansprouts, pepper
(capsicum) and spring onions. Add oil to
reserved sugar and soy sauce, then whisk in
vinegar and pour over salad. Toss lightly
together.

Serves 4-6.

ACCOMPANIMENTS

COOL AVOCADO DIP

1 ripe avocado
2 teaspoons lemon juice
155 ml (5 fl oz/⅔ cup) thick sour cream
1 teaspoon grated onion
salt and pepper
slice of lemon, to garnish

Cut avocado in half, discard stone, then scoop out flesh into a bowl. Mash flesh with lemon juice until smooth. Stir in sour cream, grated onion and season with salt and pepper. Serve chilled, garnished with a slice of lemon.

ANCHOVY MAYONNAISE

45 g (1½ oz) can anchovies
6 tablespoons mayonnaise
2 tablespoons single (light) cream
2 tablespoons olive oil
1 teaspoon tomato purée (paste)
chopped fresh parsley, to garnish

Drain anchovies and put into a blender with remaining ingredients. Blend ingredients until smooth. Serve chilled, garnished with chopped parsley.

HORSERADISH SAUCE

155 ml (5 fl oz/⅔ cup) double (thick) cream
1 tablespoon grated horseradish
2 spring onions, chopped
salt and pepper
chopped fresh chives, to garnish

In a bowl, whip cream until softly peaking, then stir in remaining ingredients and season with salt and pepper. Serve chilled, garnished with chopped chives.

ACCOMPANIMENTS

CUCUMBER YOGURT SAUCE

125 g (4 oz) low fat soft cheese
155 ml (5 fl oz/⅔ cup) natural yogurt
½ a cucumber, peeled and finely diced
2 teaspoons lemon juice
salt and pepper
chopped cucumber, to garnish

In a bowl, beat cheese and yogurt together until smooth. Add cucumber, lemon juice and season with salt and pepper. Serve chilled, garnished with chopped cucumber.

SPICY ORIENTAL SAUCE

2 tablespoons soy sauce
juice of ½ a lemon
2 fresh green chillies, seeded and chopped
1 clove garlic, crushed
2 teaspoons sesame oil

Put all the ingredients into a bowl and mix together. Serve chilled.

MUSTARD SAUCE

3 teaspoons Dijon mustard
155 ml (5 fl oz/⅔ cup) thick sour cream
3 tablespoons mayonnaise
salt and pepper
crushed mustard seeds or wholegrain mustard,
    to garnish

Put all the ingredients into a bowl and mix well together until smooth. Season with salt and pepper. Serve chilled, garnished with mustard seeds or wholegrain mustard.

CREAMY POTATO SKINS

1.5 kg (3 lb) medium potatoes
90 g (3 oz/⅓ cup) butter, melted
salt
155 ml (5 fl oz/⅔ cup) thick sour cream
2 tablespoons chopped fresh chives
chopped fresh chives, to garnish

Preheat the oven to 200C (400F/Gas 6). Scrub potatoes and prick with a fork. Bake in the oven for about 1 hour until tender.

Remove potatoes from the oven and cut each one into quarters. Carefully remove insides leaving about 0.5 cm (¼ in) of flesh on the skins. (The cooked potato can be used in soups.) Increase oven temperature to 230C (450F/Gas 8).

Brush the insides and outsides of potato skins with melted butter. Place on a baking sheet, sprinkle with salt and return to the oven for about 10 minutes or until crisp. Mix thick sour cream with chives and serve with the hot potato skins. Garnish sour cream mixture with chopped chives.

Serves 4-6.

CHINESE FRIED RICE

2 tablespoons oil
½ a bunch of spring onions, chopped
125 g (4 oz) mushrooms, chopped
½ a red pepper (capsicum), seeded and chopped
½ a green pepper (capsicum), seeded and chopped
500 g (1 lb) cooked long-grain rice, well drained
125 g (4 oz) cooked, peeled prawns
125 g (4 oz) cooked ham, diced
½ teaspoon ground ginger
¼ teaspoon cayenne pepper
salt
spring onion tassels, to garnish

Heat oil in a large frying pan, add onions, mushrooms and peppers (capsicums).

Cook for 2 minutes, then stir in cooked rice and cook for 3 minutes, stirring frequently during cooking.

Add prawns and ham to the pan, then stir in the spices and season with salt. Continue cooking for a further 3-4 minutes. Serve hot, garnished with spring onion tassels.

Serves 4-6.

SEAFOOD KEBABS

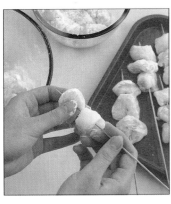

8 large scallops
625 g (1 ¼ lb) monkfish, boned
seasoned flour

TARRAGON WINE SAUCE: 30 g (1 oz/6 teaspoons) butter
1 shallot, finely chopped
155 ml (5 fl oz/⅔ cup) dry white wine
2 teaspoons chopped fresh tarragon
salt and pepper
4 tablespoons single (light) cream

Remove the coral parts from scallops and reserve. Cut white parts in half.

Cut monkfish into bite-size pieces. Toss scallops and monkfish in seasoned flour. Thread one piece of scallop and 2 pieces of monkfish onto 16 bamboo skewers and keep in refrigerator until needed. (These will be cooked in the hot oil later.)

To make tarragon wine sauce, melt butter in a saucepan. Add shallot and cook until soft, then add reserved scallop corals and cook over a gentle heat for 5 minutes. Pour in wine, add tarragon and season with salt and pepper. Simmer for 5 minutes. Purée sauce in a blender or food processor until smooth, then return to saucepan, stir in cream and reheat before serving.

Serves 4.

CRISPY COD BITES

750 g (1½ lb) thick cod fillet, skinned
seasoned flour
2 eggs, beaten
125 g (4 oz/2 cups) fresh breadcrumbs

LEMON PARSLEY SAUCE: 30 g (1 oz/6 teaspoons)
    butter
6 teaspoons plain flour
250 ml (8 fl oz/1 cup) fish stock
grated peel and juice ½ a lemon
1 tablespoon chopped fresh parsley
salt and pepper
3 tablespoons single (light) cream

Cut fish in bite-size pieces. Toss in flour, dip
in egg, then coat in breadcrumbs.

To make lemon parsley sauce, melt butter in a
saucepan, stir in flour and cook for 1 minute.
Gradually add stock, then bring to the boil
and simmer 1-2 minutes until sauce thickens,
stirring all the time. Stir in lemon peel and
juice, parsley and season with salt and pepper.
Reheat for 1 minute, then stir in cream.

Serve the sauce with the fish which is speared
onto fondue forks and cooked in the hot oil.

Serves 4-6.

Note: Serve also with Dill Sauce, see page
48, or Thousand Island Sauce, see page 49.

GEFILLTE FISH

750 g (1½ lb) mixed white fish, skinned
1 small onion, quartered
1 egg, beaten
2 tablespoons chopped fresh parsley
30 g (1 oz/¼ cup) ground almonds
4 tablespoons fine matzo meal
salt and pepper

CREAMY BEETROOT SAUCE: 155 ml (5 fl oz/⅔ cup)
  thick sour cream
60 g (2 oz) cooked beetroot, grated
1 tablespoon horseradish sauce

Coarsely mince the fish and onion
or chop in a food processor.

Add the remaining ingredients to minced fish
and mix well. (The mixture should be stiff; if
necessary add a little more matzo meal.)
With wetted hands, form mixture into 36
smooth balls. Place on a tray and refrigerate
for at least 30 minutes before cooking in hot
oil.

To make creamy beetroot sauce, put cream
into a bowl, add grated beetroot, then mix in
horseradish sauce and season with salt and
pepper.

Serves 6.

SPICY PRAWNS

750 g (1½ lb) cooked Mediterranean (king) prawns
2 tablespoons oil
1 teaspoon paprika
2 tablespoons lemon juice

PIQUANT SAUCE: 315 ml (10 fl oz/1¼ cups) tomato
   juice
2 teaspoons demerara sugar
2 teaspoons red wine vinegar
¼ teaspoon ground cinnamon
¼ teaspoon ground ginger
1 small fresh red chilli, seeded and finely chopped

Peel prawns, leaving tail shells on, if desired, and put into a bowl. Add oil, paprika and lemon juice; mix well.

Cover prawns and leave to marinate for at least 1 hour in refrigerator. To make piquant sauce, put all ingredients into a saucepan and simmer for 15 minutes.

Before heating prawns in hot oil, drain and arrange prawns on a serving plate. Reheat piquant sauce and serve with hot prawns.

Serves 6 as a starter, 4 as a main course.

Note: Raw Mediterranean (king) prawns may be used, if desired. Follow instructions given above, then cook raw prawns in hot oil for 2-3 minutes.

ALMANDINE TROUT

4 trout
seasoned flour
2 eggs, beaten
250 g (8 oz/2 cups) blanched almonds, lightly
   toasted and finely chopped

DILL SAUCE: 4 teaspoons cornflour
155 ml (5 fl oz/⅔ cup) fish stock
155 ml (5 fl oz/⅔ cup) milk
2 tablespoons chopped fresh dill
salt and pepper

Clean and bone the fish and cut off fins, then slice into pieces just under 1 cm (½ in) thick.

Toss pieces of trout first in seasoned flour, then dip in egg and finally coat in chopped almonds. Place on a serving plate and refrigerate until ready to cook in the hot oil.

To make dill sauce, in a saucepan blend cornflour smoothly with a little fish stock, then add remainder together with the milk and heat until simmering, stirring all the time. Cook for 2 minutes until thickened. Stir in dill and season with salt and pepper. Serve hot.

Serves 4.

SWORDFISH ACAPULCO

750 g (1½ lb) swordfish steaks, cut into
  bite-size pieces

MARINADE: 4 tablespoons oil
155 ml (5 fl oz/⅔ cup) dry white wine
1 clove garlic, crushed

THOUSAND ISLAND SAUCE: 1 hard-boiled egg
250 ml (8 fl oz/1 cup) mayonnaise
1 teaspoon tomato purée (paste)
2 tablespoons chopped stuffed olives
2 tablespoons finely chopped onion
salt and pepper
1 tablespoon chopped fresh parsley

Combine marinade ingredients; stir in fish.

Cover and leave fish to marinate in
refrigerator for 2-3 hours. To make Thousand
Island sauce, chop hard-boiled egg. Put all
ingredients into a bowl, season to taste with
salt and pepper and mix together. Spoon into
a serving dish.

Before cooking the fish in hot oil, drain from
marinade and arrange in a serving dish.

Serves 4.

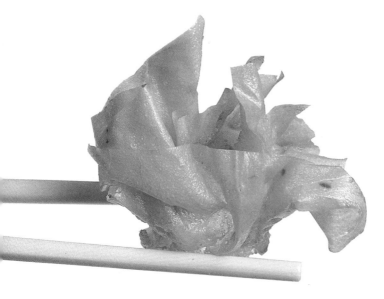

WAFER-WRAPPED PRAWNS

375 g (12 oz) peeled prawns, coarsely chopped
1 fresh green chilli, seeded and finely chopped
2 teaspoons oyster sauce
2 sheets filo pastry

CHILLI SAUCE: 4 tablespoons tomato ketchup (sauce)
1-2 teaspoons chilli sauce
½ teaspoon sesame oil

In a bowl, mix prawns, chilli and oyster sauce together.

Cut filo pastry into 10 cm (4 in) squares. Place a heaped teaspoon of prawn filling in the centre of each square, then draw the corners of the pastry together and twist them to form little bundles. Place on a floured serving plate. Cover and chill until required. (Do not make these too far in advance – as bases become soggy if left to stand for too long.) The best way to cook bundles is for each person to use a small Chinese wire strainer – this makes it easier and safer when lifting bundles out of the hot oil.

To make chilli sauce, put tomato ketchup (sauce), chilli sauce, 2 tablespoons water and sesame oil into a saucepan and heat gently for 3-4 minutes. Serve hot with the prawn bundles, as a starter.

Makes 24.

Note: Alternatively serve with Devilled Sauce, see page 29.

SEAFOOD TEMPURA

4 plaice fillets, skinned
225 g (8 oz) halibut, skinned and boned
225 g (8 oz) fresh salmon, skinned and boned
225 g (8 oz) scampi tails, thawed if frozen
4 small squid, cut into rings
1 quantity Chilli Sauce, see page 50
3 teaspoons peeled and grated fresh root
    ginger and 225 g (8 oz) daikon (mooli),
    grated, to garnish
1 quantity Batter, see page 53

Cut plaice, halibut and salmon into thin slices or fingers; arrange on a platter with scampi and squid.

Make chilli sauce. Prepare the garnish by mixing ginger and daikon (mooli) together.

Make batter. Each person spears a piece of fish, dips it into the batter, then cooks it in the hot oil. The cooked food is then dipped into the chilli sauce and eaten with the garnish.

Serves 4-6.

CAULIFLOWER FRITTERS

1 cauliflower, cut into flowerets
90 g (3 oz/¾ cup) dried breadcrumbs
45 g (1½ oz/⅓ cup) grated Parmesan cheese
1 tablespoon chopped fresh parsley
salt and pepper
2-3 eggs, beaten

CHEESE SAUCE: 15 g (½ oz/3 teaspoons) butter
15 g (½ oz/6 teaspoons) plain flour
315 ml (10 fl oz/1¼ cups) milk
½ teaspoon prepared mustard
60 g (2 oz/½ cup) grated Chedder cheese
pinch of cayenne pepper

Par-boil cauliflower in a saucepan of boiling, salted water for 4-5 minutes; drain well.

In a bowl, mix together breadcrumbs, Parmesan cheese and parsley and season with salt and pepper. Dip cauliflower flowerets in beaten egg, then coat in breadcrumb mixture. Put onto a serving plate and set aside until ready to cook in the hot oil.

To make cheese sauce, melt butter in a small saucepan, stir in flour and cook for 1 minute. Remove from heat and add milk slowly. Bring to the boil, stirring, then simmer for 2 minutes. Stir in mustard, cheese, cayenne and season with salt and pepper. Serve hot.

Serves 4-6.

Note: Alternatively serve with Piquant Sauce, see page 47.

— MIXED VEGETABLE KEBABS —

4 courgettes (zucchini), cut into slices
16 button mushrooms
1 red pepper (capsicum), seeded and cut into chunks
1 green pepper (capsicum), seeded and cut into
   chunks

CREAMY ONION SAUCE: 125 g (4 oz/½ cup) low fat
   soft cheese
155 ml (5 fl oz/⅔ cup) natural yogurt
½ a bunch spring onions, finely chopped

BATTER: 2 large eggs
125 g (4 oz/1 cup) plain flour

Thread the vegetables onto 12-16 bamboo skewers.

To make the creamy onion sauce, mix all the ingredients together and put into a serving bowl.

Just before cooking kebabs, make batter. Put eggs into a bowl with 220 ml (7 fl oz/1 cup) iced water and beat until frothy. Add flour and beat until just blended – do not worry if a few lumps are left. Pour into a bowl or jug and stand it in a bowl of ice. To cook kebabs, each person dips a skewer into the batter, then into hot oil to cook until the batter is golden. The kebabs are then eaten with the onion sauce.

Serves 4.

SPICY CHICK PEA BALLS

125 g (4 oz/¾ cup) bulgar wheat
125 ml (4 fl oz/½ cup) boiling water
225 g (8 oz/1¼ cups) chick peas, soaked overnight
2 tablespoons sunflower oil
2 cloves garlic, crushed
½ teaspoon baking powder
1 teaspoon chilli powder
1 teaspoon ground coriander
1 teaspoon ground cumin
salt and pepper

FRESH TOMATO SAUCE: 4 tomatoes, skinned
½ a green pepper (capsicum), halved and seeded
½ a red pepper (capsicum), halved and seeded
1 fresh green chilli, seeded
1 tablespoon fresh coriander, chopped

Put the bulgar wheat into a bowl, pour over the boiling water and leave the wheat to soak for 1 hour. Drain chick peas and put into a food processor with bulgar wheat and remaining ingredients, except those for fresh tomato sauce. Blend for a few minutes until mixture becomes fairly smooth. With your hands, mould the mixture into a 36 small balls and place on a serving dish. These will be speared with a fondue fork and cooked in the hot oil.

To make the fresh tomato sauce, put all the ingredients into a blender or food processor and process until vegetables are finely chopped. Add seasoning, then put into a serving bowl.

Serves 4-6.

SWISS POTATOES

1 kg (2 lb) small new potatoes, scrubbed
2 eggs, beaten
125 g (4 oz/1 cup) herb stuffing mix

GARLIC SAUCE: 125 g (4 oz/2 cups) fresh white
    breadcrumbs
2 cloves garlic
salt and pepper
250 ml (8 fl oz/1 cup) olive oil
4 teaspoons lemon juice
1 tablespoon white wine vinegar

Boil potatoes (in skins) until just tender; drain and cool. Dip in beaten egg, then roll in stuffing mix and set aside.

To make garlic sauce, dampen breadcrumbs with 1 tablespoon water. Put into a blender or food processor with garlic and ½ teaspoon salt and blend together until well mixed. Add oil a little at a time and continue to process until all the oil has been added.

Work the lemon juice and vinegar into the sauce until it forms a smooth, creamy consistency. Season with pepper. Turn mixture into a bowl and serve with the potatoes which are speared and cooked in the hot oil.

Serves 4-6.

Note: Serve the potatoes also with Cheese Sauce, see page 52.

AUBERGINE FRITTERS

500 g (1 lb) aubergines (eggplants), diced
1-2 teaspoons salt
seasoned flour

BATTER: 125 g (4 oz/1 cup) plain flour
2 eggs, separated
2 tablespoons olive oil

COOL CURRY DIP: 2 teaspoons curry paste
1 teaspoon Dijon mustard
2 teaspoons brown sugar
4 teaspoons grated onion
6 tablespoons mayonnaise
6 tablespoons natural yogurt

Put aubergine in a colander, add salt.

Leave aubergine (eggplant) to stand for 30 minutes. To make the batter, sift flour and ¼ teaspoon salt into a bowl, beat in egg yolks and oil. Gradually add 185 ml (6 fl oz/¾ cup) water and continue to beat to make a smooth batter. Leave to stand for 1 hour. Just before serving, whisk egg whites until stiff and fold into batter.

To make cool curry dip, whisk all ingredients together in a bowl, then spoon into a serving dish. Rinse aubergine under cold, running water and dry thoroughly on absorbent paper. Dust diced aubergine with seasoned flour. To cook fritters, each piece of aubergine is dipped into batter, then cooked in hot oil in the fondue pot.

Serves 4.

CANTONESE HOTPOT

225 g (8 oz) rump steak, fat removed
375 g (12 oz) skinned chicken breasts (fillets)
125 g (4 oz) mange tout (snow peas)
225 g (8 oz) peeled prawns
1 red pepper (capsicum), seeded and cut into strips
125 g (4 oz) button mushrooms, halved
225 g (8 oz) can bamboo shoots, drained
1.75 litres (3 pints/7½ cups) chicken stock
2 teaspoons peeled, chopped fresh root ginger
60 g (2 oz) fine egg noodles, broken up

YELLOW BEAN SAUCE: 1 tablespoon soy sauce
2 tablespoons yellow bean sauce
1 tablespoon dry sherry
1 fresh green chilli, seeded and finely chopped

Slice steak and chicken thinly and arrange on 6 individual plates. Top and tail mange tout (snow peas) and arrange on plates with prawns and remaining vegetables. Put stock into a large saucepan with ginger and simmer for 15 minutes. Soak egg noodles in warm water for 10 minutes, then drain and put into a serving bowl. In a bowl, combine ingredients for yellow bean sauce, then add 2 tablespoons water and divide between 6 small dishes.

Pour stock into fondue pot, bring back to simmering; place over burner. Each person uses a fondue fork (or Chinese wire strainer) to dip pieces of food into stock to cook. The cooked food is then dipped into the sauce before eating. When all the meat and vegetables have been eaten, add noodles to fondue pot to heat through, then ladle soup into bowls.

Serves 6.

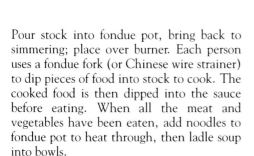

— CHINESE SEAFOOD HOTPOT —

3 lemon sole fillets, skinned
4 trout fillets, skinned
6 raw Mediterranean (king) prawns
6 scallops, sliced
4 small squid, cut into rings
1.75 litres (3 pints/7½ cups) chicken stock
1 teaspoon peeled and sliced fresh root ginger
60 g (2 oz) transparent rice noodles
4 spring onions, chopped
500 g (1 lb) spring cabbage, finely shredded

HOISIN SAUCE: 2 tablespoons hoisin sauce
1 tablespoon tomato ketchup (sauce)
2 teaspoons soy sauce

Cut sole and trout into thin strips and arrange
on a platter with the other fish. Put stock into
a pan with ginger and simmer for 15 minutes.
Mix the ingredients for hoisin sauce together
and put into 6 small dishes. Soak noodles in
warm water for 5 minutes, then cut into short
lengths and put into a serving bowl. Place
spring onions and shredded cabbage in a
bowl.

Strain stock into a fondue pot, bring back to
simmering, then place over the burner.
Arrange the platter of fish, hoisin sauce,
noodles and cabbage on the dining table. The
fish and cabbage are cooked in the hot stock
using Chinese wire strainers to hold the food.
Any remaining cabbage can be added at the
end with the noodles to make the soup.

Serves 6.

THAI MEAT & FISHBALLS

MEATBALLS: 3 dried mushrooms
500 g (1 lb) lean minced beef
1 tablespoon chopped fresh coriander
3 spring onions, finely chopped
1 tablespoon rice wine or dry sherry
salt and pepper

FISHBALLS: 100 g (3½ oz) can shrimps, drained
750 g (1½ lb) cod or haddock fillets, skinned
1 teaspoon peeled, grated fresh root ginger
3 teaspoons cornflour
1.2 litres (40 fl oz/5 cups) chicken stock

GINGER SAUCE: 2 teaspoons chopped root ginger
2 tablespoons rice wine or dry sherry
2 tablespoons Japanese soy sauce

To make the meatballs, soak dried mushrooms in cold water to cover for 30 minutes. Squeeze out water from mushrooms and chop finely. Put beef into a bowl with coriander, chopped mushrooms, onions, wine or sherry and season with salt and pepper; mix well together. With wetted hands, form mixture into 18 small balls.

To make fishballs: mince, or finely chop in a food processor, the shrimps and cod or haddock fillets. Stir in the grated root ginger, cornflour and seasoning to taste. With wetted hands, form mixture into 24 small balls. Mix together ingredients for ginger sauce and pour into a serving bowl. Bring stock to the boil in fondue pot. The meat and fish balls are cooked in hot stock, using fondue forks or Chinese wire strainers to hold the food.

Serves 6.

— GOLDEN VEGETABLE PURÉE —

225 g (8 oz) carrots
1 small turnip
½ medium swede
2 sticks celery
1 small onion
315 ml (10 fl oz/1¼ cups) chicken stock
60 g (2 oz/¼ cup) butter, diced
salt and pepper
pinch of freshly grated nutmeg
small cooked sausages and cooked potatoes, to serve

Chop all vegetables finely, then put into a saucepan with stock. Bring to the boil and simmer until just tender.

Drain vegetables and leave to cool slightly. Purée vegetables in a blender or food processor, then pass the purée through a sieve into the fondue pot.

Place the pot over a low heat and gradually beat in the butter. Season with salt, pepper and nutmeg and keep hot over the burner while dipping sausages and potatoes into vegetable mixture.

Serves 4-6.

MUSHROOM FONDUE

60 g (2 oz/¼ cup) butter
500 g (1 lb) mushrooms, finely chopped
2 cloves garlic, crushed
155 ml (5 fl oz/⅔ cup) chicken stock
155 ml (5 fl oz/⅔ cup) double (thick) cream
3 teaspoons cornflour
salt and pepper
pinch of cayenne pepper
cubes of cheese and garlic sausage, to serve

Melt butter in a saucepan, add mushrooms and garlic and cook gently for 10 minutes.

Add stock and simmer for 10 minutes. Cool slightly and purée in a blender or food processor.

Put a little cream into the fondue pot, blend in cornflour smoothly, then add remaining cream and mushroom purée. Heat to simmer and cook over a gentle heat until thickened, stirring frequently. Season with salt, pepper and cayenne. Serve with cubes of cheese and garlic sausage.

Serves 4-6.

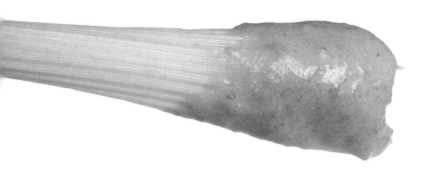

TOMATO NIÇOISE

60 g (2 oz/¼ cup) butter
750 g (1½ lb) ripe tomatoes
1 clove garlic, crushed
1 small onion, chopped
185 g (6 oz) can pimentoes, drained and chopped
salt and pepper
pinch of sugar
2 tablespoons mayonnaise
cooked artichoke leaves, cooked green beans, strips of
    cucumber and celery, to serve

Melt butter in a saucepan, add tomatoes, garlic, onion and pimento and cook gently for 10-15 minutes until soft.

Sieve mixture into a bowl; season with salt, pepper and sugar and leave to cool. Whisk in mayonnaise.

Pour the tomato niçoise into a serving bowl. Arrange the vegetables on a large platter and stand the bowl in the centre.

Serves 4-6.

LEEK PURÉE

1 kg (2 lb) leeks, coarsely chopped
155 ml (5 fl oz/²⁄₃ cup) chicken stock
60 g (2 oz/¼ cup) butter
salt and pepper
pinch of freshly grated nutmeg
2 spring onions, finely chopped
raw cauliflower flowerets, carrot sticks and
    button mushrooms, to serve

Wash the leeks well, then put into a saucepan
with 1 tablespoon water and cook for 10-15
minutes until soft.

Drain leeks and leave to cool slightly. Purée
leeks in a blender or food processor with stock
until smooth.

Spoon purée into a fondue pot. Place over a
gentle heat and beat in butter and season
with salt, pepper and nutmeg. Stir in spring
onions and keep warm on a low burner. Serve
with a selection of raw vegetables or as an
accompaniment to grilled meat.

Serves 4-6.

SWEETCORN FONDUE

500 g (1 lb) frozen sweetcorn kernels
2 teaspoons cornflour
3 tablespoons single (light) cream
salt and pepper
few drops Tabasco sauce
30 g (1 oz/6 teaspoons) butter
selection of cooked prawns and mussels, to serve

Put sweetcorn into a saucepan with 2 tablespoons water and simmer for a few minutes until tender.

Drain the corn and put into a blender or food processor and process until soft but not too smooth. In a saucepan, blend cornflour smoothly with cream. Add sweetcorn mixture and cook over a low heat until smooth.

Pour mixture into a fondue pot, season with salt, pepper and Tabasco sauce, then beat in butter. Set pot over a low burner to keep warm. Serve with a selection of cooked shellfish.

Serves 4-6.

BLACK-EYED BEAN DIP

225 g (8 oz/1 cup) black-eyed beans,
  soaked overnight in cold water
1 clove garlic
few sprigs of parsley
½ teaspoon salt
60 g (2 oz/¼ cup) butter
1 onion, chopped
1 teaspoon curry paste
155 ml (5 fl oz/⅔ cup) natural yogurt

CURRIED BREAD CUBES: 1 small white loaf
vegetable oil for frying
3 teaspoons curry powder

Drain soaking water from beans.

Add enough fresh water to cover beans, add
garlic and parsley and simmer for about 1
hour until beans are tender. Stir salt into
beans and cook for a further 5 minutes; drain
and discard parsley. In a small saucepan, melt
butter, add onion and cook until tender. Put
beans and onion into a blender or food
processor and blend until puréed. Put bean
purée into a fondue pot, stir in curry paste and
yogurt and reheat.

To make curried bread cubes, cut crusts off
loaf, then cut bread into cubes. Heat oil in a
frying pan and fry bread cubes until crisp and
golden, then drain on absorbent kitchen
paper. Sprinkle with curry powder and toss
together. Spear bread cubes with fondue forks
and dip into bean fondue to eat.

Serves 4-6.

STRAWBERRY ROULÉ DIP

440 g (14 oz) can strawberries, drained
250 g (8 oz) strawberry roulé cheese
155 ml (5 fl oz/²⁄₃ cup) double (thick) cream
fresh strawberries and Quick Almond Sponge,
    see page 69, to serve

Put strawberries and cheese into a blender or
food processor and blend until smooth.

In a bowl, whip the cream until softly
peaking, then fold in the strawberry cheese
mixture. Turn mixture into a serving bowl.

Hull strawberries, if desired, and arrange on a
serving plate with cubes of almond sponge.
Spear a strawberry or a piece of sponge on
fondue forks and dunk in the dip.

Serves 4-6.

RASPBERRY CREAM

500 g (1 lb) raspberries, thawed if frozen
4 teaspoons cornflour
315 ml (10 fl oz/1¼ cups) single (light) cream
60 g (2 oz/⅓ cup) icing sugar
3 tablespoons Framboise, if desired

QUICK MERINGUES: 2 egg whites
125 g (4 oz/⅔ cup) icing sugar

Rub raspberries through a sieve and discard seeds. Keep purée on one side.

To make the meringues, preheat oven to 160C (325F/Gas 3). Line a baking sheet with non-stick paper. Place egg whites and icing sugar in a bowl over a pan of hot water and with an electric whisk, whisk until mixture is stiff and standing in peaks. Place mixture in a piping bag fitted with a 1 cm (½ in) star nozzle and pipe small blobs onto lined baking sheet. Bake in the oven for 10-15 minutes until crisp on the outside. Allow to cool before removing from paper.

In a saucepan, blend the cornflour smoothly with a little of the cream. Stir in the remainder and add sugar and raspberry purée. Cook over a gentle heat until smooth and thickened. Stir in the Framboise, if desired, then pour into a fondue pot and serve with small meringues. Serve hot or cold.

Serves 4-6.

SPICED PLUM PURÉE

750 g (1½ lb) red or yellow plums
90 g (3 oz/½ cup) sugar
½ teaspoon ground cinnamon
4 teaspoons cornflour
2 tablespoons ginger wine
Lemon Sponge, see page 105, and slices of apple
    and pear, to serve

Cut plums in half; discard stones. Put plums into a saucepan with sugar and cinnamon and 315 ml (10 fl oz/1¼ cups) water. Cover and simmer for 15 minutes.

Press the fruit mixture through a sieve into a fondue pot.

In a small bowl, blend cornflour smoothly with wine and stir into plum purée. Heat gently, stirring until thickened. Serve with small squares of lemon sponge and slices of apple and pear to dip into the purée.

Serves 4-6.

APRICOT YOGURT DIP

225 g (8 oz) semi-dried apricots
2 tablespoons Amaretto liqueur
155 ml (5 fl oz/²⁄₃ cup) natural yogurt

QUICK ALMOND SPONGE: 2 eggs
125 g (4 oz/¹⁄₂ cup) soft tub margarine
125 g (4 oz/¹⁄₂ cup) caster sugar
125 g (4 oz/1 cup) self-raising flour
pinch of baking powder
few drops almond essence

Put apricots into a bowl, cover with 315 ml (10 fl oz/1¹⁄₄ cups) water and leave to soak for 2-3 hours.

To make quick almond sponge, preheat oven to 180C (350F/Gas 4). Grease a 17.5 cm (7 in) shallow, square cake tin. Put all the ingredients for sponge into a bowl and beat with a wooden spoon for 3 minutes. Turn mixture into greased tin and bake in the oven for 25 minutes or until golden brown and firm to the touch. Turn onto a wire rack and leave to cool. Cut into small squares when cold.

Drain apricots (reserving liquor) and put into a blender or food processor with the Amaretto and yogurt. Blend until smooth. If mixture is a little too thick, add a small amount of reserved apricot liquor. Spoon into a fondue pot and heat over a burner to serve warm (or serve cold) with the pieces of cake.

Serves 4-6.

— GOOSEBERRY WINE FONDUE —

750 g (1½ lb) gooseberries, topped and tailed
125 g (4 oz/½ cup) caster sugar
155 ml (5 fl oz/⅔ cup) dry white wine
2 teaspoons cornflour
2 tablespoons single (light) cream

BRANDY SNAPS: 60 g (2 oz/¼ cup) butter
125 g (4 oz/⅓ cup) demerara sugar
125 g (4 oz/2 tablespoons) golden syrup
125 g (4 oz/½ cup) plain flour
½ teaspoon ground ginger

To make brandy snaps, preheat oven to 180C (350F/Gas 4). Melt butter, sugar and golden syrup in a saucepan.

Cool slightly, then beat in flour and ginger. Place 4 teaspoonfuls of mixture onto a baking sheet, spaced well apart, and bake in the oven for 10 minutes. Repeat with remaining mixture, to make a total of 24. Leave each batch to cool slightly on baking sheet before removing with a palette knife and rolling around clean, greased pencils or chopsticks. Allow to cool and set before removing.

Put gooseberries into a saucepan with sugar and wine. Simmer until tender. Reserve a few gooseberries for decoration, then pass remainder through a sieve to make a purée. In a fondue pot, blend cornflour smoothly with cream. Stir in gooseberry purée, then heat until smooth and thick, stirring frequently. Decorate with reserved gooseberries and serve with brandy snaps.

Serves 4-6.

— BLACKCURRANT FONDUE —

750 g (1½ lb) blackcurrants, topped and tailed if fresh;
   thawed if frozen
125 g (4 oz/½ cup) caster sugar
3 teaspoons cornflour
2 tablespoons single (light) cream
4 tablespoons Cassis

HAZELNUT MACAROONS: 2 egg whites
125 g (4 oz/½ cup) light soft brown sugar
185 g (6 oz/1⅔ cups) ground hazelnuts
30 g (1 oz/¼ cup) finely chopped hazelnuts

To make macaroons, preheat oven to 180C
(350F/Gas 4). Line 3 baking sheets with
non-stick paper. Whisk egg whites until
softly peaking. Fold in sugar and ground nuts.

Place spoonfuls onto lined baking sheets to
make a total of 24. Sprinkle with chopped
nuts and bake in the oven for 15-20 minutes
until crisp and firm to the touch.

To make the fondue, put blackcurrants into a
saucepan with sugar and 155 ml (5 fl oz/⅔
cup) water and cook gently until tender. Press
mixture through a sieve into a fondue pot. In
a small bowl, blend cornflour smoothly with
cream and stir into the purée together with
Cassis. Reheat until thickened, stirring
frequently. Serve with hazelnut macaroons.

Serves 4-6.

Note: Swirl a little extra cream in to serve, if
desired.

BUTTERSCOTCH FONDUE

60 g (2 oz/¼ cup) butter
125 g (4 oz/¾ cup) demerara sugar
4 tablespoons golden syrup
440 g (14 oz) can evaporated milk
4 tablespoons chopped unsalted peanuts
6 teaspoons cornflour
pieces of apple, pear and banana
    and popcorn, to serve

Put butter, sugar and golden syrup into a saucepan and heat gently until mixture begins to bubble, stirring occasionally. Allow to boil for 1 minute.

Stir in evaporated milk and cook for 3-4 minutes until sauce is hot and bubbling, then add chopped nuts.

In a small bowl, blend cornflour smoothly with 2 tablespoons water. Add mixture to sauce in pan and heat until thickened, stirring. Pour into a fondue pot and place over a burner to keep warm. Serve with pieces of apple, pear and banana and popcorn.

Serves 4-6.

PEPPERMINT FONDUE

625 ml (20 fl oz/2½ cups) single (light) cream
155 g (5 oz/1 cup) icing sugar
6 teaspoons cornflour
peppermint essence, to taste

MINI CHOCOLATE CAKES: 2 eggs
125 g (4 oz/½ cup) soft tub margarine
125 g (4 oz/½ cup) caster sugar
125 g (4 oz/1 cup) self-raising flour
6 teaspoons cocoa
3 teaspoons milk

To make chocolate cakes, preheat oven to
190C (375F/Gas 5). Put all ingredients into a
bowl and beat together until smooth.

Put teaspoonfuls of mixture into 40 petits fours
cases on a baking sheet. Bake in the oven for 15
minutes until cooked. Leave to cool on a wire
rack before removing from paper cases.

Put cream and sugar into a saucepan and heat
gently until almost boiling. Blend cornflour
smoothly with 1 tablespoon water, add to
cream and continue to heat, stirring all the
time until thickened. Add essence, to taste,
then pour into a fondue pot and serve hot
with mini chocolate cakes.

Serves 6.

— CHOCOLATE NUT FONDUE —

375 g (12 oz) Swiss chocolate with nuts
250 ml (8 fl oz/1 cup) double (thick) cream
2 tablespoons brandy or rum
a selection of fresh fruit, to serve

VIENNESE FINGERS: 125 g (4 oz/½ cup) butter
30 g (1 oz/2 tablespoons) icing sugar
125 g (4 oz/1 cup) plain flour
¼ teaspoon baking powder
few drops vanilla essence

To make Viennese fingers, preheat oven to 190C (375F/Gas 5). Grease 2 or 3 baking sheets. Beat butter and icing sugar together in a bowl until pale and creamy.

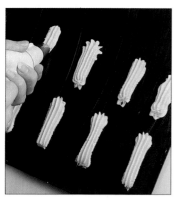

Add sifted flour, baking powder and vanilla essence and beat well. Put mixture into a piping bag fitted with 0.5 cm (¼ in) star nozzle and pipe 5 cm (2 in) fingers onto greased baking sheets, to make a total of 24. Bake in the oven for 15 minutes. Leave to cool on a wire rack.

To make chocolate fondue, break up chocolate into a fondue pot. Add cream and heat gently, stirring all the time until chocolate melts. Stir in brandy or rum, then leave over a burner to keep warm. Serve with Viennese fingers and fruit.

Serves 6.

— MOCHA TIA MARIA FONDUE —

225 g (8 oz) plain (dark) chocolate
3 teaspoons instant coffee powder
155 ml (5 fl oz/⅔ cup) double (thick) cream
3 tablespoons Tia Maria
a selection of fresh fruit, to serve

NUTTY MERINGUES: 2 egg whites
125 g (4 oz/½ cup) caster sugar
60 g (2 oz) flaked almonds, lightly toasted

To make meringues, preheat oven to 110C (225F/Gas ¼). Line 2 or 3 baking sheets with non-stick paper. Whisk egg whites until stiff, then fold in half the sugar and whisk again until stiff. Lightly fold in remaining sugar.

Put teaspoonfuls of mixture onto lined baking sheets to make a total of 30. Insert a few almonds into each one, then bake for 1½-2 hours until dry and crisp. Turn off oven, but leave meringues in oven to cool. Peel meringues off paper once they are cool.

To make mocha fondue, break up chocolate into a fondue pot, add coffee and cream and heat gently until melted, stirring all the time. Stir in Tia Maria and beat until smooth. Leave pot over a burner to keep warm. Serve with nutty meringues and fruit.

Serves 6.

PRALINE FONDUE

125 g (4 oz/½ cup) caster sugar
125 g (4 oz/¾ cup) blanched almonds
225 g (8 oz) white chocolate
155 ml (5 fl oz/⅔ cup) double (thick) cream
few drops vanilla essence
cubes of cake and a selection of fresh fruit, to serve

To make praline, oil a baking sheet. Put sugar and almonds into a small heavy-based saucepan. Place over a low heat and leave until sugar becomes liquid and golden. Pour at once onto oiled baking sheet, then leave to cool and harden for 15 minutes.

Coarsely break up praline, then put into a blender or food processor amd process until finely ground.

Put chocolate and cream into a fondue pot and heat gently until chocolate melts, stirring all the time. Stir in praline and flavour with a few drops of essence. Serve with cubes of cake and pieces of fresh fruit.

Serves 6.

FRUIT SURPRISES

375 g (12 oz) frozen puff pastry, thawed
250 g (8 oz) can pineapple slices, drained and
  juice reserved
60 g (2 oz/⅓ cup) glacé cherries, chopped
30 g (1 oz) angelica, chopped

RUM SAUCE: **4 oranges**
3 teaspoons cornflour
60 g (2 oz/⅓ cup) demerara sugar
30 g (1 oz/6 teaspoons) butter, diced
4 tablespoons dark rum

Roll out pastry thinly on a lightly floured surface to a large square, then cut into eighteen 7.5 cm (3 in) squares.

Chop pineapple and mix with cherries and angelica. Place a teaspoonful of mixture in the centre of each pastry square. Dampen the edges with water and fold over to form triangles; seal well and fork the edges. Refrigerate until needed. The pastry triangles are cooked when required, in hot oil in the fondue pot. Once cooked, lift from hot oil, using Chinese wire strainers, if possible.

To make rum sauce, finely grate peel from one of the oranges, then squeeze juice from all of them. Put cornflour in a saucepan, add reserved pineapple juice and blend together smoothly. Add sugar and orange juice and stir well. Bring to the boil, stirring all the time and simmer for 2 minutes. Whisk in butter, orange peel and rum. Serve hot with the hot pastry triangles.

Serves 6.

FRUIT FRITTERS

2 bananas, cut into 2.5 cm (1 in) pieces
2 eating apples, cored and cut into chunks
2 teaspoons lemon juice
1 small, fresh pineapple, skinned and cut into chunks
125 g (4 oz/½ cup) caster sugar mixed with
    1 teaspoon ground cinnamon, to serve

BATTER: 125 g (4 oz/1 cup) plain flour
pinch of salt
1 egg
155 ml (5 fl oz/⅔ cup) milk

Toss bananas and apples in lemon juice, then arrange on a plate with pineapple.

To make batter, sift flour and salt into a bowl. Beat in egg, then gradually add milk, beating to make a smooth batter.

The fritters are cooked at the table by spearing the fruit with a fondue fork, dipping it in the batter and cooking in hot oil. Pat each fritter on absorbent kitchen paper, then dip in cinnamon sugar mixture before eating.

Serves 6.

Note: To add extra colour, decorate cinnamon sugar with a sprig of mint or pineapple leaves, if desired.

HOT BERRY COMPOTE

500 g (1 lb) mixed summer fruits such as redcurrants,
blackcurrants and raspberries
125 g (4 oz/½ cup) caster sugar
pinch of mixed spice
6 teaspoons cornflour

LANGUE DE CHAT BISCUITS: 125 g (4 oz/½ cup) butter
125 g (4 oz/½ cup) caster sugar
2 eggs
185 g (6 oz/1½ cups) self-raising flour

To make biscuits, preheat oven to 220C (425F/
Gas 7). Grease 2 or 3 baking sheets. Beat butter
and sugar together until pale and fluffy; beat in
eggs and work in flour.

Put mixture into a piping bag fitted with a 1
cm (½ in) plain nozzle and pipe 6 cm (2½ in)
fingers onto greased baking sheets (spaced
well apart) to make a batch of 24-30. Bake in
the oven for about 8 minutes until light
golden. Cool on a wire rack.

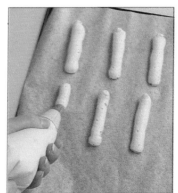

To make fondue, put fruits into a saucepan
with sugar and 155 ml (5 fl oz/⅔ cup) water
and cook gently until tender. Crush fruits
slightly with a potato masher and add mixed
spice. In a small bowl, blend cornflour
smoothly with a little water. Add to fruit in
pan and cook until thickened, stirring all the
time. Pour into a fondue pot and place over a
burner. Serve with langue de chat biscuits.

Serves 6.

SWEET CHERRY COMPOTE

two 470 g (15 oz) cans red cherries
6 teaspoons cornflour
90 g (3 oz/⅓ cup) caster sugar
3 tablespoons cherry brandy
ice cream, to serve

FANCY CAKES: **60 g (2 oz/¼ cup) butter**
2 eggs, separated
60 g (2 oz/¼ cup) caster sugar
60 g (2 oz/½ cup) plain flour
grated peel of ½ a lemon

To make cakes, preheat oven to 190C (375F/ Gas 5). Grease and flour 12 bun tins. Warm butter in a pan until just melting.

Whisk egg yolks and sugar until pale and creamy. Lightly fold in sifted flour, lemon peel and butter until thoroughly mixed. Whisk egg whites until stiff and fold into mixture. Spoon mixture into greased and floured bun tins. Bake in the oven for 10 minutes or until golden and firm to touch. Turn out and cool on a wire rack.

To make the compote, drain cherries, reserving juice, and remove stones. In a saucepan, blend cornflour smoothly with a little of the reserved juice, then add the remainder and stir in sugar. Cook over a medium heat until the sauce has thickened, stirring all the time. Stir in cherries and brandy. Reheat, then pour into the fondue pot. Serve with a small ladle to pour over ice cream and fancy cakes.

Serves 6.

— MARSHMALLOW FONDUE —

6 teaspoons cornflour
470 ml (15 fl oz/2 cups) single (light) cream
185 g (6 oz) packet marshmallows

CRISPY CAKES: 60 g (2 oz/¼ cup) butter
2 tablespoons golden syrup
60 g (2 oz/½ cup) drinking chocolate
90 g (3 oz) rice breakfast cereal

To make crispy cakes, put 60 petits fours cases on 2 baking sheets. Place butter and syrup in a saucepan and stir over a low heat until melted. Remove from heat and stir in drinking chocolate and rice cereal, mixing well until thoroughly coated.

Using a teaspoon, spoon the mixture into petits fours cases and refrigerate until set.

To make marshmallow cream, in a saucepan blend cornflour smoothly with a little cream, then stir in remainder and add marshmallows. Cook over a gentle heat until mixture thickens and marshmallows melt, stirring all the time. Pour into a fondue pot. Serve hot with the crispy cakes.

Serves 6-8.

COCONUT DIP

90 g (3 oz/1 cup) desiccated coconut
60 g (2 oz) creamed coconut, chopped
60 g (2 oz/¼ cup) sugar
4 teaspoons cornflour
155 ml (5 fl oz/⅔ cup) single (light) cream

MINI FLAPJACKS: 125 g (4 oz/½ cup) margarine
4 tablespoons clear honey
90 g (3 oz/½ cup) soft brown sugar
250 g (8 oz/2 cups) porridge oats
60 g (2 oz/⅓ cup) chopped blanched almonds

To make flapjacks, preheat oven to 180C (350F/Gas 4). In a saucepan, melt margarine, honey and sugar. Add oats and nuts; mix well.

Using a teaspoon, spoon mixture into 48 petits fours cases on a baking sheet. Bake in the oven for 20 minutes until golden. Leave to cool.

To make dip, put desiccated coconut in a saucepan with 500 ml (16 fl oz/2 cups) water, the creamed coconut and sugar. Bring to the boil and simmer for 10 minutes. Strain mixture into a bowl, pressing mixture thoroughly to extract all liquid. In a fondue pot, blend cornflour smoothly with cream, then add coconut liquid and cook over a gentle heat until thickened, stirring all the time. Serve warm with mini flapjacks.

Serves 6.

SABAYON SAUCE

4 large, ripe, firm eating pears
125 ml (4 fl oz/½ cup) Marsala
3 egg yolks
90 g (3 oz/⅓ cup) caster sugar
3 teaspoons brandy

Preheat oven to 180C (350F/Gas 4). Peel, halve and core pears and slice thickly. Put in an ovenproof dish, pour over Marsala, then cover and bake in the oven for 20 minutes.

Drain off juice from pears and reserve. Place egg yolks and sugar in a bowl and whisk until pale and frothy. Add reserved juice from pears, then place bowl over a pan of simmering water and whisk until mixture is thick.

Remove bowl from pan, stir in brandy and serve immediately, with the pear slices for dipping.

Serves 4-6.

SHRIMP DIP

220 g (7 oz) can shrimps, drained
125 g (4 oz/½ cup) cream cheese
4 tablespoons mayonnaise
1 small clove garlic, crushed
1 tablespoon white wine
1 teaspoon lemon juice
1 tablespoon chopped fresh chives
small savoury crackers, to serve

Finely chop the drained shrimps.

In a bowl, beat together cream cheese and mayonnaise until smooth. Add the garlic, wine and lemon juice and mix well.

Stir in the shrimps and chives, then spoon mixture into a serving bowl. Serve chilled with small crackers.

Serves 6.

AÏOLI WITH CRUDITÉS

4 cloves garlic
¼ teaspoon salt
2 egg yolks
315 ml (10 fl oz/1¼ cups) olive oil
3 teaspoons lemon juice
pepper
a selection of fresh vegetables, to serve
chopped fresh parsley, to garnish

In a bowl, crush garlic cloves with salt to form a pulp. Stir in egg yolks and beat well.

Gradually beat in the olive oil, drop by drop, beating vigorously all the time. When the mayonnaise starts to become creamy and smooth, add the oil in a thin, steady trickle and continue beating until the aïoli is thick. Stir in lemon juice and season with pepper.

Spoon aïoli into a serving bowl and place in the centre of a serving platter. Cut the vegetables into thin strips or chunks and arrange them around the bowl of aïoli. Garnish aïoli with chopped parsley before serving.

Serves 6.

GUACAMOLE

2 ripe avocados
3 tablespoons lime juice
1 clove garlic, crushed
2 tomatoes, skinned and finely chopped
3 spring onions, finely chopped
1 fresh green chilli, seeded and finely chopped
1 tablespoon chopped fresh coriander leaves
salt and pepper
corn or tortilla chips, to serve
sprig of coriander, to garnish

Cut avocados in half, remove stones and scoop out flesh into a bowl. Mash together with lime juice.

Add garlic, chopped tomatoes, spring onions, chilli, coriander and season with salt and pepper.

Spoon into a bowl and surround with the corn or tortilla chips. Garnish with a sprig of coriander.

Serves 6.

Note: This dip is best made just before serving.

TAPENADE DIP

125 g (4 oz) black olives, stoned
50 g (1¾ oz) can anchovies, rinsed and drained
2 tablespoons capers
2 teaspoons lemon juice
2 teaspoons brandy
½ teaspoon Dijon mustard
4 tablespoons olive oil
sprig of parsley, to garnish
fingers of toast, to serve

Put olives, anchovies, capers, lemon juice, brandy and mustard into a blender or food processor and process until smooth.

Gradually add the olive oil to the puréed mixture in a steady stream to give a smooth consistency.

Spoon mixture into a serving dish. Garnish with a sprig of parsley. Serve with fingers of toast.

Serves 6.

BAGNA CAUDA

two 50 g (1¾ oz) cans anchovies, drained
3 cloves garlic
185 g (6 oz/¾ cup) butter
6 tablespoons olive oil
pepper
a selection of raw or cooked vegetables and breadsticks,
    to serve

Put anchovies into a bowl with garlic and mash well to make a paste. Alternatively, put ingredients into a blender or food processor and work to a purée.

Heat butter and oil in a saucepan until melted. Whisk into the anchovy paste to give a smooth consistency. Season with pepper.

Pour mixture into a small fondue pot or special Bagna Cauda pot. Serve with a selection of fresh vegetables and breadsticks.

Serves 6.

CRAB & CHEESE DIP

125 g (4 oz) low fat soft cheese
60 g (2 oz/½ cup) finely grated Chedder cheese
1 teaspoon lemon juice
few drops Tabasco sauce
1 tablespoon tomato ketchup (sauce)
3 tablespoons single (light) cream
220 g (7 oz) can crabmeat, drained and flaked
sprig of dill, to garnish

CHEESE TWISTS: 125 g (4 oz/1 cup) plain flour
pinch of salt, cayenne and dry mustard
60 g (2 oz/¼ cup) margarine, diced
60 g (2 oz/½ cup) grated mature Chedder cheese
1 egg yolk
beaten egg, to glaze
grated Parmesan cheese for sprinkling

Mix together all ingredients for dip. Turn mixture into a serving bowl and chill. To make the cheese twists, sift dry ingredients into a bowl and rub in margarine finely. Stir in cheese. Beat egg yolk with 1 tablespoon water, add to mixture and mix to form a dough. Knead lightly, then chill for 30 minutes.

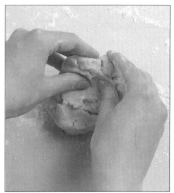

Preheat oven to 200C (400F/Gas 6). Grease 2 or 3 baking sheets. Roll out dough on a lightly floured surface to a 0.5 cm (¼ in) thick rectangle. Brush with egg to glaze and sprinkle with Parmesan cheese. Cut into strips measuring 0.5 cm (¼ in) wide and 10 cm (4 in) long to make a total of 40. Twist both ends of each strip and place on greased baking sheets. Bake in the oven for 10-12 minutes until golden. Cool on a wire rack. Serve with dip, garnished with a sprig of dill.

Serves 6.

MONGOLIAN HOTPOT

1.5 kg (3 lb) lean lamb, leg or fillet
1.75 litres (3 pints/7½ cups) chicken stock
1 teaspoon peeled, grated fresh root ginger
1 clove garlic, crushed
2 tablespoons chopped spring onion
2 tablespoons chopped fresh coriander
125 g (4 oz) spinach leaves, shredded
225 g (8 oz) Chinese leaves, shredded
90 g (3 oz) instant soup noodles

HOTPOT DIPPING SAUCE: 6 tablespoons soy sauce
3 tablespoons smooth peanut butter
2 tablespoons rice wine or dry sherry
pinch of chilli powder
3 tablespoons hot water

Slice lamb very thinly and arrange on two large plates. Put stock into a large saucepan with ginger and garlic and simmer for 15 minutes. Put spring onion, coriander, spinach, Chinese leaves and noodles into separate serving bowls. Combine the ingredients for dipping sauce and divide between 6 small dishes.

Put stock into a special Mongolian hotpot or a fondue pot. Add spring onions and bring back to boil. Transfer pot to burner. Each person uses fondue forks, or Chinese wire strainers, to cook pieces of food in stock. The food is then dipped in sauce before eating. Any remaining spinach and Chinese leaves are finally added to the pot with coriander and noodles. When noodles are tender the soup is served in bowls.

Serves 6.

SAVOURY PARCELS

60 g (2 oz/¼ cup) butter
2 shallots, finely chopped
185 g (6 oz) lean bacon, chopped
500 g (1 lb) chicken livers, trimmed and chopped
225 g (8 oz) mushrooms, chopped
8 tablespoons chicken stock
2 egg yolks
pinch of mixed dried herbs
salt and pepper
3-4 sheets filo pastry
1 egg white

Melt the butter in a large frying pan, add shallots and cook for 2 minutes.

Add bacon and cook for 3-4 minutes. Stir in chicken livers and cook for 3 minutes, then add mushrooms and cook for 3 minutes. Pour stock into pan and simmer until it has almost evaporated. Cool slightly, then stir in egg yolks, herbs and season with salt and pepper. Put mixture in a blender or food processor and chop coarsely. Leave to cool.

Cut pastry into eighteen-twenty four 15 cm (6 in) squares. Place a tablespoon of chicken liver mixture at one end of each square. Fold over each side, then roll up parcel so it resembles a spring roll. Seal the edges with egg white, then set aside until needed. The parcels are cooked in hot oil in the fondue pot, using Chinese wire strainers for cooking and lifting parcels from hot oil.

Serves 6.

CHICKEN GOUJONS

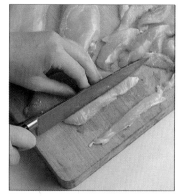

750 g (1½ lb) boneless, chicken breasts, skinned
seasoned flour
3 eggs, beaten
90 g (3 oz/¾ cup) dry breadcrumbs

RED PEPPER SAUCE: 30 g (1 oz/6 teaspoons) butter
1 small onion, chopped
2 red peppers (capsicums), seeded and chopped
1 clove garlic, crushed
250 ml (8 fl oz/1 cup) chicken stock
salt and pepper
sprig of dill, to garnish

Cut chicken into long strips about 1 cm
(½ in) wide.

Dust with seasoned flour, dip in egg, then
coat with breadcrumbs. Place in refrigerator
to chill. To make red pepper sauce, in a small
saucepan melt butter, add onion and cook
until soft. Add red peppers (capsicums) and
garlic and continue to cook over a gentle heat
for 5 minutes. Pour in stock and simmer for
10 minutes or until peppers (capsicums) are
tender.

Sieve red pepper sauce, season with salt and
pepper and reheat. Serve with chicken
goujons which are cooked in the hot oil in the
fondue pot. Garnish sauce with a sprig of dill.

Serves 6.

CRUNCHY CAMEMBERT

twelve 30 g (1 oz) portions Camembert
2 eggs, beaten
125 g (4 oz/1 cup) dried breadcrumbs

BLUEBERRY SAUCE: 2 teaspoons cornflour
225 g (8 oz) blueberries, thawed if frozen
60 g (2 oz/¼ cup) sugar
pinch of freshly grated nutmeg
2 teaspoons lemon juice
sprig of mint, to garnish

Freeze the Camembert portions for 1 hour. Dip each cheese portion in egg, then in breadcrumbs. Dip portions again in egg and crumbs. Put on a plate; chill until needed.

To make blueberry sauce, in a saucepan blend cornflour smoothly with 90 ml (3 fl oz/⅓ cup) water. Add remaining ingredients and simmer until the liquid thickens, stirring all the time. Serve warm.

The Camembert portions are cooked in hot oil in fondue pot at the table, using Chinese wire strainers if possible to lift them out of the pot (fondue forks will pierce the crust and cause cheese to ooze out). Serve with the sauce. Garnish with a sprig of mint.

Serves 6.

—— TURKEY CRANBERRY DIP ——

375 g (12 oz) sugar
500 g (1 lb) fresh cranberries
2 tablespoons port
1 kg (2 lb) cooked, diced turkey or chicken, to serve

In a large saucepan, put sugar and 470 ml (15 fl oz/2 cups) water. Heat gently, stirring to dissolve sugar, then boil for 5 minutes.

Add cranberries and simmer for about 10 minutes until skins pop.

Remove from heat and stir in port. Pour mixture into fondue pot. Serve with diced turkey or chicken for dipping.

Serves 6.

PROVENÇAL MEATBALLS

750 g (1½ lb) minced beef
1 small onion, finely chopped
60 g (2 oz) stuffed olives, finely chopped
1 small egg, beaten
salt and pepper
plain flour, for coating

PROVENÇAL DIP: 1 aubergine (eggplant), diced
3 tablespoons olive oil
1 shallot, finely chopped
1 clove garlic, crushed
500 g (1 lb) tomatoes, skinned and chopped
1 tablespoon tomato purée (paste)
1 tablespoon chopped fresh parsley

Sprinkle aubergine (eggplant) for dip with salt and drain for 30 minutes. In a bowl, mix together ingredients for meatballs, except flour. With wetted hands, roll mixture into 36 small balls, then coat in flour. Chill in refrigerator until needed.

To make dip, rinse aubergine (eggplant) and pat dry. Heat oil in a large saucepan and cook shallot and garlic gently for 2 minutes. Add aubergine (eggplant) and cook gently for 10 minutes. Add tomatoes and purée (paste), cover and cook for a further 5-8 minutes until vegetables are almost reduced to a pulp. Stir in parsley and seasoning . Serve warm with the meatballs which are cooked in hot oil in the fondue pot.

Serves 6.

CHOW MEIN SALAD

125 g (4 oz) Chinese medium egg noodles
125 g (4 oz) mange tout (snow peas)
185 g (6 oz) fresh beansprouts
½ a bunch of spring onions, chopped
1 red pepper (capsicum), seeded and sliced
125 g (4 oz) button mushrooms, sliced
1 small Little Gem lettuce, shredded

DRESSING: 4 tablespoons sunflower oil
2 tablespoons lemon juice
3 teaspoons soy sauce
2.5 cm (1 in) piece of fresh root ginger
2 tablespoons sesame seeds

Break up noodles and cook in boiling, salted water for 5-6 minutes.

Drain noodles and leave to cool. Top and tail mange tout (snow peas), then break in half and put into a bowl. Pour over enough boiling water to cover and leave to stand for 2 minutes; drain and cool. Put noodles and mange tout (snow peas) into a salad bowl and add remaining salad ingredients.

In a bowl, combine oil, lemon juice and soy sauce. Peel and cut ginger into very thin slivers and add to bowl. Mix ingredients well together and pour over salad. Toss well together. Sprinkle with sesame seeds just before serving.

Serves 6-8.

— SUMMER VEGETABLE SALAD —

375 g (12 oz) aubergine (eggplant), diced
salt and pepper
3 tablespoons olive oil
1 Spanish onion, sliced
375 g (12 oz) courgettes (zucchini), sliced
1 red pepper (capsicum), seeded and cut into chunks
1 green pepper (capsicum), seeded and cut into chunks
1 yellow pepper (capsicum), seeded and cut into chunks
3 tomatoes, skinned and chopped
1 tablespoon chopped fresh basil
1 tablespoon chopped fresh parsley, if desired

Put aubergine (eggplant) into a colander, sprinkle with salt and leave to stand for 30 minutes. Rinse, drain and pat dry.

Heat oil in a large frying pan, add aubergine (eggplant) and onion and cook over medium heat for 5 minutes. Add courgettes (zucchini) and peppers (capsicums); cook over a low heat for 15 minutes, turning occasionally until tender.

Transfer vegetables to a bowl, stir in tomatoes, basil and seasoning. Leave to cool, then chill. Serve sprinkled with chopped parsley, if desired.

Serves 6.

POTATO SALAD

750 g (1½ lb) new potatoes, scrubbed
½ a bunch of spring onions, chopped
1 tablespoon chopped fresh parsley
1 teaspoon chopped fresh marjoram
1 tablespoon chopped fresh dill
sprigs of marjoram, to garnish

YOGURT DRESSING: 5 tablespoons natural yogurt
3 tablespoons mayonnaise
2 teaspoons lemon juice
1 teaspoon Dijon mustard
salt and pepper

Cook potatoes in boiling, salted water until tender; drain and leave to cool.

Slice potatoes thickly and put into a serving bowl. Reserve a little of the chopped spring onions and fresh herbs for garnishing. Add remaining onions and fresh herbs to potatoes in bowl and toss together lightly until combined.

Mix together ingredients for yogurt dressing. Pour over the salad and mix lightly. Serve chilled, garnished with reserved chopped spring onions and chopped fresh mixed herbs and sprigs of marjoram.

Serves 6.

MIXED LEAF SALAD

½ a head each of 2 different types of lettuce
  such as cos, webb's, iceberg, oakleaf
1 avocado
2 teaspoons lemon juice
1 green pepper (capsicum), seeded and sliced
½ a cucumber, sliced
½ a bunch of spring onions, chopped
watercress, trimmed
curly endive
3 sticks celery, chopped

DRESSING: 6 teaspoons walnut oil
6 teaspoons sunflower oil
3 teaspoons white wine vinegar
½ teaspoon Dijon mustard
salt and pepper

Put lettuce into a large salad bowl. Halve the
avocado, remove the stone, then peel. Cut
flesh into slices and coat with lemon juice,
then add to bowl. Add remaining salad
ingredients.

In a bowl, mix together dressing ingredients.
Pour over the salad and toss lightly until
thoroughly coated with dressing.

Serves 6-8.

CARIBBEAN COLESLAW

1 red-leafed lettuce, such as oakleaf
½ an iceberg lettuce, shredded
5 sticks celery, finely sliced
185 g (6 oz) carrots, grated
½ a small pineapple, cut into chunks
90 g (3 oz) fresh dates, stoned and chopped
60 g (2 oz) walnuts or pecans, chopped

DRESSING: 3 tablespoons mayonnaise
finely grated peel and juice of 1 lime
6 teaspoons sunflower oil
salt and pepper

Line a large salad bowl or platter with red-leafed lettuce.

In a bowl, put the remaining salad ingredients, except the nuts, and mix together. Mix dressing ingredients together, then pour over salad and toss lightly.

Spoon salad into the prepared bowl or onto the platter and sprinkle with walnuts or pecans before serving.

Serves 6.

RICE & SPINACH SALAD

375 g (12 oz/2½ cups) long-grain rice
2 tablespoons oil
1 bunch spring onions, chopped
225 g (8 oz) frozen chopped spinach, thawed and well
   drained
salt and pepper
slice of lemon, to garnish

In a medium saucepan, bring 1 litre (32 fl oz/4 cups) salted water to the boil. Keep water simmering while adding rice, then cover and cook for 15 minutes until rice is soft and water absorbed.

In a large saucepan, heat oil, add onions and cook for 3-4 minutes, then stir into rice.

Add spinach and season with salt and pepper, then heat through for 1-2 minutes. Stir ingredients together and serve warm, garnished with a slice of lemon. (Alternatively serve the rice cold and fluff up with a fork before serving.)

Serves 6.

── GRAPEFRUIT MELON DIP ──

1 Honeydew melon
2 large grapefruit
6 teaspoons sugar
6 teaspoons Galliano
3 teaspoons cornflour
6 teaspoons double (thick) cream
sprig of mint, to garnish

Cut melon in half, scoop out seeds, then using a melon ball cutter, cut out as many balls as possible, then put in a serving dish.

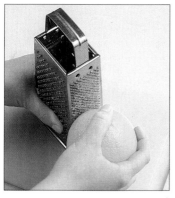

Finely grate enough peel from grapefruit to yield 1 teaspoon, then squeeze juice from both grapefruit. Put sugar, Galliano and cornflour into a saucepan and blend smoothly together. Stir in grapefruit juice and peel, then bring to the boil, stirring all the time and simmer for 1 minute.

Remove from heat, stir in cream and pour into a serving bowl. Garnish with a sprig of mint and serve warm with the melon balls to dip into the sauce.

Serves 6.

— FROTHY CHAMPAGNE DIP —

3 eggs
60 g (2 oz/¼ cup) caster sugar
finely grated peel ½ an orange
155 ml (5 fl oz/⅔ cup) double (thick) cream
155 ml (5 fl oz/⅔ cup) Champagne or medium dry
   white sparkling wine
fresh strawberries and cubes of Quick
   Almond Sponge, see page 69, to serve

Put eggs, sugar and orange peel into a bowl.
Stand bowl over a saucepan of hot water and
whisk until mixture is thick and fluffy.

Remove bowl from pan and whisk in cream
and Champagne or wine.

Pour sauce into a warmed serving bowl or
glass dish. Serve with strawberries and cubes
of almond sponge.

Serves 6.

HOT FUDGE ICES

250 ml (8 fl oz/1 cup) double (thick) cream
90 g (3 oz/⅓ cup) butter
60 g (2 oz/⅓ cup) soft brown sugar
vanilla and chocolate ice cream and 125 g (4 oz)
    chopped almonds, lightly toasted, to serve

At least 2 hours before serving the meal prepare the ice cream. Soften the ice cream slightly, then, using an ice cream scoop, make small vanilla and chocolate scoops. Place scoops on a baking sheet and coat with nuts, then quickly return ice cream to the freezer.

To make the fudge sauce, heat cream and butter in a heavy-based saucepan over a low heat until butter has melted, stirring all the time.

Add sugar and continue stirring until sugar has dissolved and mixture comes to the boil. Boil for 2 minutes until thick and glossy. Serve with the ice cream scoops.

Serves 6.

— DRAMBUIE CREAM FONDUE —

4 teaspoons cornflour
315 ml (10 fl oz/1¼ cups) double (thick) cream
3 teaspoons caster sugar
3 tablespoons Drambuie
3 oranges, peeled and segmented, to serve

LEMON SPONGE: 2 eggs
125 g (4 oz/½ cup) soft tub margarine
125 g (4 oz/½ cup) caster sugar
125 g (4 oz/1 cup) self-raising flour
pinch of baking powder
finely grated peel and juice ½ a lemon

Preheat oven to 180C (350F/Gas 4). Put all
ingredients for sponge in a bowl.

Beat together for 3 minutes. Grease a 17.5 cm
(7 in) shallow, square cake tin. Turn
mixture into greased cake tin. Bake in the
oven for 25 minutes or until golden and firm
to the touch. Turn onto a wire rack and leave
to cool. Cut into small squares when cold.

To make fondue, in a saucepan, blend
cornflour smoothly with cream. Cook over
gentle heat until thickened and smooth,
stirring all the time. Stir in sugar and
Drambuie, then pour into a serving dish.
Serve with segments of orange and squares of
lemon sponge.

Serves 6.

Note: Cut the peel from oranges into strips to
decorate, if desired.

— SAUCY ORANGE BEIGNETS —

60 g (2 oz/¼ cup) butter
155 g (5 oz/1½ cups) plain flour, sifted
3 large eggs, beaten
few drops vanilla essence
30 g (1 oz/5 teaspoons) caster sugar
vegetable oil for deep frying
extra caster sugar, to finish

ORANGE SAUCE: 4 large oranges
2 lemons
4 teaspoons arrowroot
knob of butter
90 g (3 oz/⅓ cup) sugar

To make orange sauce, finely grate peel from 2 oranges and 1 lemon.

Squeeze juice from all the oranges and lemons. In a saucepan, blend arrowroot smoothly with a little of the fruit juice, then add remainder. Stir in 155 ml (5 fl oz/⅔ cup) water and bring to the boil. Simmer 1 minute, stirring all the time. Stir in orange and lemon peel, butter and sugar and simmer for 2 minutes. Keep warm while making beignets.

Put butter in a pan with 315 ml (10 fl oz/1¼ cups) water. Bring to the boil. Off the heat, add flour and beat until smooth. Gradually beat in eggs, essence and sugar. Heat oil in a deep fat fryer to 180C (350F) or until a day-old cube of bread browns in 60 seconds. Drop teaspoonfuls of paste into oil, a few at a time. Cook for 6-8 minutes until golden. Drain and dust with sugar. Keep warm while cooking remainder. Place sauce in fondue pot on burner. Serve with hot beignets.

Serves 6.

CREAMY KIWI DIP

3 kiwi fruit, peeled
375 g (12 oz) fromage fraise
3 teaspoons caster sugar

MELTING MOMENTS: 125 g (4 oz/½ cup) butter
85 g (3 oz/⅓ cup) caster sugar
1 egg yolk
few drops vanilla essence
155 g (5 oz/1¼ cups) self-raising flour
30 g (1 oz/1 cup) crushed cornflakes

To make melting moments, beat butter and
sugar together until light and fluffy. Beat in
egg yolk and essence, then gradually work in
flour to make a stiff dough.

Chill for 15 minutes. Preheat oven to 190C
(375F/Gas 5). Grease 2 or 3 baking sheets.
Divide dough into 30 small balls and lightly
press each one into crushed cornflakes. Place
on greased baking sheets, spacing well apart.
Bake in the oven for 15 minutes or until
golden brown. Cool on a wire rack.

To make kiwi dip, put peeled kiwi fruit into a
bowl and mash with a fork. Stir in fromage
fraise and sugar and mix well. Spoon into a
serving bowl and serve with melting
moments.

Serves 6.

MENU ONE

Shrimp Dip, see page 84

◆

Mongolian Hotpot, see page 90

◆

Chow Mein Salad, see page 96

◆

Grapefruit Melon Dip, see page 102

MENU TWO

Aïoli with Crudités, see page 85

◆

Savoury Parcels, see page 91

◆

Summer Vegetable Salad, see page 97

◆

Frothy Champagne Dip, see page 103

MENU THREE

Guacamole, see page 86

◆

Chicken Goujons, see page 92

◆

Potato Salad, see page 98

◆

Hot Fudge Ices, see page 104

MENU FOUR

Tapenade Dip, see page 87

◆

Crunchy Camembert, see page 93

◆

Mixed Leaf Salad, see page 99

◆

Drambuie Cream Fondue, see page 105

MENU FIVE

Bagna Cauda, see page 88

◆

Turkey Cranberry Dip, see page 94

◆

Caribbean Coleslaw, see page 100

◆

Saucy Orange Beignets, see page 106

MENU SIX

Crab & Cheese Dip, see page 89

◆

Provençal Meatballs, see page 95

◆

Rice & Spinach Salad, see page 101

◆

Creamy Kiwi Dip, see page 107

INDEX